# JUPIT

A new look at accepted concepts of Jupiter's function in the natal chart.

# JUPITER

## An Astrologer's Guide

*by*

## EVE JACKSON

THE AQUARIAN PRESS
Wellingborough, Northamptonshire

First published 1986

© EVE JACKSON 1986

British Library Cataloguing in Publication Data

Jackson, Eve
  Jupiter: the astrological anatomy of a
  planet.
  1. Jupiter (Planet)    2. Astrology
  I. Title
  133.5'3    BF1724.2.J8

ISBN 0-85030-487-3

*The Aquarian Press is part of the
Thorsons Publishing Group*

Printed and bound in Great Britain

# Contents

# Acknowledgements

I would like to thank David Hamblin for his contributions, Graham Ellis and Olivia Barclay for their lively correspondence on the subject of Jupiter, David Fisher, creator of the Astrological Association data bank, for the speedy supply of accurate data — any chart errors will be *despite* his assistance — Pat Harris, most of whose painstaking research on Jupiter transits is not mentioned in the book due to my own error, and Cambridge University Press for their kind permission to reproduce the vase painting of Zeus and Semele first published by A. B. Cook in his monumental work *Zeus*.

I am also indebted to those teachers, colleagues, clients and students over the years, whose thoughts and experiences have filtered through me into this book, and to Dave Stevens, for his unfailing supply of support and encouragement.

The Astrostar programmes produced by Astro-Graphics are responsible for most of the calculations, run on an Osborne computer.

**Note**
All charts are drawn with Placidus house cusps.

# Introduction

Writing a book on Jupiter has not been without its difficulties. In the first place one can never truly isolate a single figure from the astrological pantheon as each is part of an interactive system, and when discussing a whole chart, focus on a single planet necessarily becomes diffused. Then there is something about the nature of this particular planet which makes it especially difficult to pin down. More experienced astrologers than myself have embarked on the task of producing a Jupiter book without succeeding in bringing it fully from the Jupiterian realm of potential, where all things are possible and one is free to follow unlimited new themes, into the finite and concrete form of printed matter. In my case the idea of writing the book came when Jupiter was passing through my third house, but once he had moved out the enthusiasm abated, and it was under the pressure of transiting Saturn in the third that I managed, tardily and grindingly, to give the book form.

If I have dwelt rather on the less attractive aspects of Jupiter it is because — as I am not the first to remark — there has been a certain coyness among astrologers in discussing them, and I feel it is time to restore the balance. We call him the Great Benefic, and we like to think he can do no wrong, particularly when he is strongly placed in our own charts, but I do not think that 'benefic' can be equated with morally good.

Some areas of Jupiterian concern have perhaps been neglected. I have not devoted much space to his more fun-loving side, which gets frequent enough report, and have scarcely mentioned sport. I feel the 'sporty' side of Jupiter and his sign Sagittarius has been rather overemphasized, and that Mars probably contributes more in this area. I hope sport enthusiasts will forgive me.

As a natal astrologer my aim has been to explore the way we experience the planet in our lives, with respect first and foremost to the birth horoscope, and as far as I am concerned this is fundamentally a psychological issue, for I perceive that what we experience as happening to us we have generally, consciously or unconsciously, drawn to ourselves. Nevertheless, the connection between inner and outer is mysterious, and we cannot be made responsible for all eventualities, except perhaps on the basis of karma from past lives. Although much of what passes as good fortune is the product of a certain kind of attitude to life, I cannot dismiss altogether the connection between Jupiter and sheer good luck.

I am still at a loss as to why Ptolemy should have regarded Jupiter as temperate, for though he is not always excessive, he is no respecter of boundaries, and that is one of his great virtues and at the same time his great danger.

Compelling though it is to try to reduce the nature of a planet to a single keyword, I have always found astrological symbolism to be rather more rounded than this, so that each planet seems to have a halo of attributes, some of them contradictory. In studying Jupiter I have been particularly struck by the way words that relate to sight have kept cropping up — vision, view, theory, speculation, seer — all of which relate to seeing at a distance. The closest I can get to an all-purpose definition of Jupiter's function — and it does not tell the whole story — is that he has to do with the urge to look or go beyond what is given and free ourselves from the limitations of the immediate situation.

# 1.
# Myth

Mythology is a psychology of antiquity . . . We moderns have
no mythology, properly speaking, but we have psychological
systems, the speculative theories about human in relation with
more-than-human forces and images, today called fields,
instincts, drives, complexes. [1]

A large part of Greek myth is politico-religious history. [2]

Every culture has its stories, which incorporate both historic
development and continuing human experience, our past being
inevitably intertwined with and contributory to our present.
Horoscopes tell stories too. We can never grasp the essentially
dynamic interplay of forces which compose a human being and are
reflected in the birth chart if we see astrological symbols in purely
static terms, as lists of immutable characteristics. The stories that
unfold with transits and progressions are never wholly novel, but
laden with millennia of biological and cultural evolution, as we
re-enact with small variations and innovations the lives of our
ancestors.

Since I am shortly to write of the Goddess, let me take the maternal
symbolism associated with the sign of Cancer as an example.
Motherhood begins with the mysterious symbiosis in which womb
and foetus are inseparable, moves through the crisis of birth into
the active feeding, holding, educative role necessary for the infant's
survival and on through its gradually diminishing dependency to
eventual detachment, so that the child is allowed to grow away and
even reject the mother as it takes over responsibility for its own life.
We do a disservice to the sign of Cancer if we refer merely to its 'caring
and protective' nature, as if motherhood were frozen in the image

of Mary, forever seated with the new-born infant in her tender arms.
Persephone's dark transformation from maid into mother, Niobe's
overweening maternal pride, Demeter's lament over the loss of her
daughter, who is the youthful aspect of herself, Jocasta's incestuous
relationship with Oedipus, and the oppressive devouring maternal
dragon that the hero has to slay are all aspects of mothering which
enrich our understanding of the sign.

Two main streams of mythology predominate in our culture, the
Judaeo-Christian and Graeco-Roman, though other strands too, such
as Celtic and Norse, play a less well-publicized role. The Christian
myth has obviously enjoyed pride of place, but as Christianity has
largely eschewed astrology and in no way incorporated planetary
symbolism, it has no traditional associations to offer the astrologer,
though we may of course make our own connections. The planets
are still known by the counterparts of the names Ptolemy knew them
by, and it is to the myths associated with these Greek names that
I primarily turn for elucidation, in particular to the stories of Zeus.

The study of mythology, however, is a slippery business. The stories
vary according to time and place, modified by local traditions,
merging with other stories. As cultures spread, mix and change, the
gods too merge with other gods, and the figure of Zeus is no
exception. There was a cult of Zeus Ammon in Egypt and a cult
of Zeus Adad which incorporated the Syrian king of gods. The temple
of Jerusalem became a temple of Zeus, and in Christian Greece he
seems to have become identified with Elijah through various
similarities. As Zeus Chthonios he was indistinguishable from deadly
Hades. He was associated variously with the ram, the bull, the wolf,
the goat, even the snake, and his numerous often contradictory
epithets run into hundreds, often relating to local variations in his
worship.[3] As he acquired the stature of god of gods, so he increasingly
took on the attributes of his rivals.

In the last analysis there is no firm line between one god or one
story and another. Myths come into being, evolve, change and
disappear, and deities likewise. And when we turn to astrology we
are scarcely on firmer ground. While the association of gods to planets
in astrology is clearly not arbitrary, neither is it stable, once and for
all. The names of the planets in Mesopotamia changed several times
as different sets of gods with different attributes took over, before
the Greeks related them to their own pantheon,[4] and the Greeks
simply allotted the planets to those deities that seemed most

nearly equivalent to the Babylonian figures. In this way Marduk, named after the current king of the Babylonian gods, became Zeus or Dias to the Greeks and later Jupiter to the Romans. The physical planets have presumably remained in the same orbits, but over the centuries and from culture to culture the human perspective on reality has evolved and changed, and the values attributed to both deities and planets have undergone corresponding changes. Nevertheless there is a central core to the symbolism of Jupiter stretching back as far as our knowledge goes, and a central core to the multiplicity of Zeus myths. At the very least we must acknowledge as much synchronicity in the Greeks' choice of names for the planets they knew as we find in the naming of recently discovered planets such as Pluto, whose chillingly appropriate name was originally proposed by an 11-year-old girl and caught on in the face of considerable competition.[5]

As far back as we can go into the development of religion in Greece, and indeed in a much wider area, we come to the era of the Great Goddess who, in her various forms, presided over the mysteries of birth, fertility and death. Typically she was worshipped as a trinity of maid, mother and crone, or goddess of the upper realm, the fruitful earth and the terrible place beneath, or the three seasons of spring, summer and winter. Her face was reflected in the three faces of the moon — the slim crescent full of promise, the mature, light-giving orb, the fear-provoking disappearance into darkness — whose cycle provided the earliest means of measuring time. The Goddess recognized obligation to no male figure, and mated freely with those of her choice. Sacred prostitution was part of her cult. Her children were hers alone, for the role of the male in procreation had not yet been understood, or at least not acknowledged.

Little is known about social organization during the period when the goddess held sway, and it is debated whether there was *matriarchy* (mother-rule) as well as *matrilatry* (mother-worship). However, numerous stories bear witness to the role of the queen/priestess, who chose an annual lover, a king for the year, who was sacrificed at the year's end, symbolizing the annual cycle of fertility and the power of the sun, to be renewed each year, and corresponding to the lovers of the Goddess such as Ishtar's beloved Tammuz. Marduk, the god associated by the Babylonians with the planet Jupiter, a local tribal deity whose fortunes grew with those of his city, appears to have been such a god. He developed from a vegetation god to a solar god, and

eventually became supreme, king of gods, gathering to himself the
titles of other gods, as also did Zeus. Annual burial rites were carried
out at Marduk's tomb, and his big festival was held at the Spring
Equinox, the Babylonian new year, when the strength of the sun
returned. One of his names (Asar) was linked to that of the grain
goddess.

Marduk may then have been originally subordinated to the local
version of the Goddess, before developing into a ruler in his own
right. Similarly, it is claimed,[6] the role of king, traditionally a solar
role, slowly freed itself from the cycle of sacrifice and the domination
of the sacred queen.

The tribes who spoke the Indo-Aryan tongues, whose origins are
unknown, had developed a male military aristocracy and worshipped
male gods, and in waves of invasions conquered and intermarried
with the more southerly goddess-worshippers. This is the story of
Greece during the second millennium before Christ. With the
Hellenes came Zeus and other masculine gods, the claim of paternity
and male authority, and the recognition of redeeming spirit,
subduing nature and exalted over matter. At first these invading gods
were subordinated to the Goddess, and possibly shared power with
her for a while, but eventually they took pride of place.

The myths of Zeus describe both this outer historical development
and the inner psychological development — the emergence of the
dominant principle of the patriarchal era which came about during
the age of Aries. In the new age social organization (represented by
Zeus) began to counterpoint blood ties (championed by Hera, his
consort), the spiritual opposed the biological, a new kind of moral
law challenged the ancient laws of nature.

Although Zeus is a sky god (see below) he is much less remote than
his grandfather Ouranos (= sky). He is still opposed to the darker,
more mysterious deities of earthy Nature. Like his counterparts in
other Aryan traditions, he is associated with mountains, and in horary
astrology Jupiter is said to rule high places. Yahweh also delivers his
precepts from a mountain top. But though a mountain may reach
to the sky it rises up from the earth. Even Olympus is made of earth's
substance, and Zeus, like Yahweh, is not above involvement with
the affairs of earthly mortals. He is even described as interbreeding
with them.

Zeus is generally depicted as a man of middle years, bearded and
imposing, wearing his *aegis* or goatskin of divine power and his cloak,

sometimes sky-blue, sometimes the deep blue of the night sky, spangled with stars. Among his many titles are King, Saviour, Father, Descender, Kindly One, Friend, Giver of Completeness, God of Marriage, Protector of Strangers, Counsellor, Cloud-Gatherer, Thunderer, Protector of Oaths.

The Greeks called him Father Zeus, and his Latin name Jupiter also incorporates the word 'father'. Most of the Olympian deities are his children, and he also fathered many heroes. He is the patriarch of Olympus, and has some features in common with 'our Father in Heaven', the Old Testament Yahweh. He is the spiritual father and triumphant paternity, following the matriarchal period when the role of father was ignored or repressed. Although he is strictly speaking not the father of men in general there is one story in which he is creator of mankind, and his fatherly role is often generalized to include mankind, Homer regularly referring to him as 'father of men and gods'.

The sure-fire way in which offspring result from his various one-off unions demonstrates the over-valuation of the male contribution to fertility, as the goddess's power was snatched away. Likewise during the Argonauts' brief stopover on the isle of Lemnos it is related that Herakles (Hercules) mated with fifty women in a sexual binge, impregnating each one. The female partner was assumed by such myths to be ever-ready for fertilization, the role of her monthly cycle now in turn overlooked. With the denial of her contribution to conception went the denial of her blood lineage.

> The common belief was that genetic inheritance resided in the male seed, the female providing little more than a passive matrix, as Apollo affirms in Aeschylus' Eumenides; and indeed the function of the ovum in mammalian genetics was not understood until the nineteenth century. A family could therefore be truly perpetuated only in the male line. [7]

In the *Eumenides* Apollo excuses Orestes' act of matricide on the grounds that his mother is not a true blood-relative:

> The mother is not the true parent of the child
> Which is called hers. She is a nurse who tends the growth
> Of young seed planted by its true parent, the male. [8]

Indeed, one of the principal themes of the Oresteian Trilogy is precisely the conflict between the old rights of motherhood and the

new law of the patriarchy. The common fancy that mares were
fertilized by the wind seems to hover somewhere between a belief
in spontaneous conception and the notion of impregnation by the
subtle power of the male. Ptolemy's statement that Jupiter rules the
fertilizing winds[9] (Marduk is also referred to as 'the god of the good
wind'[10]) surely constitutes a link between these two views. And he
is not wrong astrologically; the image of the sower of seeds is one
that again and again seems appropriate when talking of Jupiter's
activity in the chart, scattering, broadcasting, casually setting new
life and new ideas into motion, and sometimes literally corresponding
with biological conception. Rain also fertilizes, and as a sky god Zeus
was also lord of rainbearing clouds, an image preserved in his descent
on Danae as a shower of fertilizing gold. (Danae, now demoted to
the status of a mortal woman, had been an agricultural goddess.)

Zeus, 'for centuries a mere demi-god, not an immortal Olympian
deity',[11] came to be the supreme god of the Greeks, so central to
their theology that classical scholars have referred to a monotheistic
tendency within the polytheistic system. (Marduk too rose to
supremacy from humble origins.) The name Zeus and the Roman
counterpart, Jupiter, both have their origins in the Indo-European
root *djeu-* or *div-*, from which we also have such words as *dieu* and
*divine*,and Zeus came to be virtually synonymous with God (as
opposed to god), his numerous epithets corresponding to the
multitudinous manifestations of the divine, thus in our astrological
system he comes to rule the ninth house, that of religion in general.

*Djeu-* means to lighten, and Zeus has generally been taken to
mean 'the bright sky', the shining god of the heavens, who gathers
the clouds, sends the fertilizing rain and terrifies with his flashes
of lightning. While he is certainly to be associated with the sky and
the fiery *aither* above it, Kerenyi[12] points out that this may not have
been the original significance of his name, as linguistically the word
does not denote an object (something bright) but rather an event,
a lighting up or illuminating.

Quoting the closing line from Sophokles' *Trachiniai*, 'and nothing
of all this [the tragic self-burning of Herakles] is not Zeus' he
concludes: ' . . . for the normal Athenian of the Classical period
. . . Zeus was the "meaning" that lighted up more or less every great
happening.'[13] This insight brings us close to the function of Jupiter
in the birth chart, for as lord of the ninth house it is precisely the
pursuit of meaning that he is concerned with. This is the dimension

of life that rescues us from the eternal blind round of nature.

Zeus's weapon is the thunderbolt, which he looses when enraged. It is shared by the Vedic Indra, another swashbuckling Aryan sky-god and rain-bringer who parallels the Greek Zeus, and also has a counterpart in Nordic mythology in the hammer of Thor.[14] Again it crops up as an attribute of Marduk, the counterpart of Zeus in the Babylonian astrological system.[15] Associated with the astrological new year in the spring, he was god of spring rain and thunder.

The thunderbolt, or *vajra*, survives in Hinduism and in the Vajrayana tradition of Tibetan Buddhism as a symbol of irresistible spiritual power and the indestructible state of being that lies beyond illusion and corruptibility. It is a masculine symbol, in tantric practices paired with a (feminine) bell. It can illuminate or destroy and points to Zeus's function as an enlightener, at the same time reminding us that he is a powerful figure, and the planet Jupiter not so harmless as he is sometimes made out to be. Homer describes him as 'unconquerable Zeus, who has brought down the high towers of many a city and will destroy others yet'.[16] Yahweh too is often associated with thunder and lightning. They announce his presence at Mount Sinai before Moses receives the ten commandments (Exodus xix, 16), and embody his wrathful power: 'The voice of the thunder was in the heaven: the lightnings lightened the world: the earth trembled and shook' (Psalm 77, 18); 'The adversaries of the Lord shall be broken to pieces; out of heaven shall he thunder upon them.' The oak, the tree sacred to Zeus (in one of the earliest shrines of Zeus, in the spectacular mountain scenery of Dodona, the oracle was read from the movement of the wind in the oak leaves), is the tree most frequently blasted by lightning.

Zeus's bird, the eagle, like lightning, brings destruction from the skies, and its remote mountain habitat makes it a suitable associate of the god. Yahweh himself is sometimes identified with the eagles: 'I bore you on eagle wings and brought you unto myself.'

Zeus is the son of Kronos (Saturn) and Rhea, Kronos being perhaps a god still subservient to the Goddess.[17] Because of a prophecy that Kronos would be forced to relinquish his throne as king of the gods to one of his children, he makes a practice of devouring them at birth. With the help of Ouranos and Gaia, Kronos's parents, whom he has overthrown in his turn, Rhea gives birth to Zeus in Crete and has him brought up there, presenting Kronos with a stone to swallow in place of his son. In due course Zeus enlists the aid of his first wife,

Metis (= Wisdom, Good Counsel), daughter of Okeanos and Tethys, who advises him to visit Rhea and ask to be made Kronos' cup-bearer. Rhea gives him a potion and, again on Metis' advice, he mixes this with his father's drink, whereupon the old god regurgitates Zeus's siblings, Hestia, Demeter, Hera, Hades and Poseidon, who under Zeus's leadership wage war upon the Titans. These older sisters and brothers, the sisters coming first, are clearly earlier deities now rearranged under the authority of Zeus. As is always the case in myths, there are different accounts of the manner in which Zeus deals with Kronos when he has fulfilled the prophecy by overthrowing the old man with the aid of his brothers and sisters. Some say he flung Kronos into the depths of Tartaros, but in other versions he is said to have banished him to a dignified exile in the Isles of the Blessed in the Western Ocean. Though prone to fits of rage and capable of meting out severe punishments, Zeus was not such a vindictive deity as, for example, Apollo. However, when threatened with a similar overthrow by an unborn son of his marriage with Metis he resorts to the same tactic as his father, swallowing his wife whole.

The future king of Olympus was born in a dark Cretan cave and nursed by the nanny-goat goddess Amaltheia. Some stories relate that he had as his foster-brother Pan the goat, or Aigipan,[18] an ancient nature deity. Other nurses mentioned are the Ash-nymphs Adrasteia and Io, daughters of Melisseus, King of Crete or Bee-god, a masculine form of Melissa (= bee, feminine). Adrasteia ('the inescapable') was the dark form of mother Rhea, and Io a bovine form of the Goddess. 'Bee' is also one of the names of the Goddess, and it was believed that all honey came from the moon,[19] and as well as being seen as a vital nutrient it was also associated with death. In some versions of the story Zeus' nurse is a sow, another of the Goddess' beasts. Nurtured on milk and honey, the infant grows in preparation for his feats of conquest.

Having overthrown his father and the other Titans, Zeus leads the Olympians in their successful war against the giants, in which they are helped by the Ekatontocheires, three giants each with a hundred arms who had been imprisoned in the depths of the earth by Kronos. His next achievement is the defeat of the monster Typhon, from the story of which he emerges as a prototype of the dragon-slaying hero. Typhon is a huge, smothering beast with a hundred serpent heads, who bays like a dog, both serpent and dog being associated with the triple-faced Moon Goddess. This embodiment of the dark, instinctual, unconscious forces is overcome by the

defender of the light and consciousness. The story has parallels in
Thor's defeat of the Midgard Worm, Indra's slaying of Vritra and
Yahweh's punishment of the serpent in the garden. Babylonian
Marduk came to power after slaying the dragon Tiamat, embodiment
of the water chaos from whom he and the other gods had sprung. [20]

It is worth noting, however, that once again Zeus only succeeds
in his task with the aid of a creature of the instinctual forces being
subdued, in this case Aigipan the goat god, just as he has usurped
his Titan parents with the help of the Titaness Metis and a retinue
of mother-figures and conquered the giants, children of Gaia, with
help from her other giant offspring, the hundred-armed

ZEUS CHASING SEMELE

Ekatontocheires. All these stories of assistance tell us that Zeus's
authority is achieved and maintained only by an alliance, albeit one-
sided, with the deities of an earlier, more biologically orientated

period, ultimately with 'the bounteous goddess Earth, . . . the mother
and nourisher of life and receiver of the dead for rebirth'.[21] His
thunder and lightning are themselves presents from the Cyclopes,
sons of Ouranos and Gaia. Semele, a goddess reduced to the status
of an unfortunate paramour of Zeus, once herself wielded the
thunderbolt to kill her son Dionysos at the annual summer solstice
sacrifice. Moira or the Moirai — Fate or the Fates — are seen as being
beyond the power of Zeus until later times when he comes to
incorporate *themis,* natural law, i.e. he assimilates Themis, another
of his wives. (Marduk also siezes the Tablets of Fate, which in that
version of the story had originally belonged to the sea-goddess Tiamat,
from the breast of her chosen husband, Kingu.[22]) Metis (swallowed,
you may remember, by Zeus) provides him with good advice from
within his belly. If there is a lesson to be drawn from this for astrology
perhaps it is that Jupiter's power, though great, has its limitations,
and needs to be grounded and nourished by the feminine principle.
Certainly he is less dangerous when allied with the feminine, and
his exaltation in Cancer suggests that such an alliance is indeed
fortunate. The biblical Yahweh, on the other hand, is much more
insistently one-sided, turning his face firmly against feminine power.

Among Zeus's divine marriages are those to Eurynome,
Mnemosyne, Metis, Thetis, Themis, Dione, Nemesis, Demeter and
Persephone, all of them great goddesses of the earth or sea, the
feminine elements of earth and water. From these unions come
numerous offspring, also largely consisting of more ancient figures,
such as Athene,[23] now brought within the domain of the new
religion, much as earlier deities have been incorporated into the
Christian congregation of saints. The stories of Zeus's many marriages
are accounts of as many rapes, or at least of deceitful seductions,
rape being the most concrete representation of the violation of the
feminine principle, and as such a common dream motif.

Better known by far than all the above-mentioned marriages is
the union of Zeus with his sister, the 'oxe-eyed' Hera. There are stories
of his pursuit and abduction of Hera — he tricks her into pity by
disguising himself as a pathetic cuckoo and then forces himself upon
her — and of a prolonged clandestine relationship with her, but
many more stories relate to his status as a married man, forever in
pursuit of one-night stands, with his vengeful wife always hot on
his heels. It is helpful to our understanding of the astrological Jupiter
to bear in mind that for Zeus the chase is everything, and long-term

commitment irksome. But the marriage of Hera endures — the
hostility of the jealous wife apparently provides Zeus with some sort
of necessary grounding, a constraint which whets his appetite for
an endless sequence of brief affairs with goddesses, nymphs and
mortal women. Thus the freewheeling Jupiterian always exists against
the background of and in contrast to a more settled and confining
way of life, and derives support from it.

Much devotion was given in antiquity to the *hieros gamos* (divine
wedding) of Zeus and Hera. Kerenyi [24] refers to the cults which centred
on the marriage bed of Hera, herself represented by a wooden doll,
to whom Zeus came as an 'invisible bridegroom'. This recalls the
image of Christ as the bridegroom and God as the Beloved of the
Sufis — it is a metaphor for the receptive devotee penetrated by the
experience of the divine. But Esther Harding, in her book *The Way
of All Women*, [25] warns against seduction by the 'ghostly lover' animus
who lures women away from the real world into a realm of fantasy.
Here we begin to touch on one of the dangers of Jupiter perhaps
more to be feared than his hurling of occasional thunderbolts, namely
his propensity for promising to unite us with the 'spiritual' and save
us from the discomforts and triviality of the 'real'. He is the seductive
aspect of the masculine principle, whether in a man's or a woman's
chart, but ultimately the attempt to fly unfettered into the realm
of the Jupiterian is prone to lead to a split, and we are driven back
to revalue the 'real' or natural in search of wholeness.

In the course of his various seductions, Zeus resorts to the most
ingenious disguises, mating in the forms of mortal men, animals
and even inanimate objects. He is as tricky in this respect as Hermes
(Mercury), that other traditional lord of the mutable signs. And he
is always successful — not only in his seduction, but also in producing
offspring from these one-night adventures. He sows his seed and
is gone, but like a Jupiter transit it requires nurturing to bring it
to fruition.

The mythological figure of Zeus thus incorporates a number of
features which are highly relevant to the role of Jupiter in astrology.
He is associated with the concept of the 'divine' in general, with
brightness, illumination and meaning, with the masculine (elements
of fire and air) as opposed to the feminine (earth and water), but
seems to require some support from the latter to achieve his ends.
He is a powerful authority figure who rages and punishes when angry,
and he is also a fickle seducer, and a rapist. He sows his seed far and
wide.

The structure of the Zeus myths shows similiarities not only with other gods worshipped by people of the Indo-European or Aryan language group (Indra, Thor), but also with the semitic Yahweh and Marduk. Despite the claim that Marduk's characteristics and story were largely concocted by the priests of Babylon to raise their deity to match the growing worldly importance of their city, they possess recognizable features in common with the Olympian deity, and the identification of his planet with Zeus does not seem too wide of the mark. Whether there was a direct connection in terms of influence, or whether the same archetypal motifs occurred independently is at present a matter of conjecture.

## Notes

1.  James Hillman: *The Dream and the Underworld*, Harper & Row, 1979.
2.  Robert Graves: *The Greek Myths*, Penguin, 1960, Vol. I, p. 17. (First published 1955).
3.  See A. B. Cook: *Zeus,* Vol. I. Cambridge University Press, 1914.
4.  Michael Baigent's forthcoming book on Babylonian astrology should supply more information on this.
5.  For an account of the naming of Pluto, see William Graves Hoyt: *Planets X and Pluto,* University of Arizona Press, 1980, pp. 215ff.
6.  See Robert Graves: *The Greek Myths,* Vol. I, p. 14.
7.  L. P. Wilkinson: *Classical Attitudes to Modern Issues,* William Kimber, 1979.
8.  Aeschylus: *The Oresteian Trilogy,* trans. Philip Vellacott, Penguin, 1959 (1956).
9.  Ptolemy: *Tetrabiblos,* trans. F. E. Robbins, Harvard University Press and William Heinemann (Loeb Classical Library), 1940, p. 37.
10. Bouché-Lecletcq: *L'Astrologie Grecque*, Paris, 1899.
11. Graves: *The Greek Myths,* Vol. I, p. 18.
12. C. Kerenyi: *Zeus and Hera: Archetypal Image of Father, Husband and Wife,* Princeton University Press, 1975, p. 9.
13. Ibid., pp. 19—20.
14. Joseph Campbell: *The Masks of God: Occidental Mythology,* Viking Press, 1964, Chapter 9.
15. Jean Bottéro: *La Religion Babylonienne*, Presses Universitaires de France, 1952, p. 59.

16. Homer: *Iliad,* Book 2. Penguin edn, trans. E. V. Rieu, 1950, p. 43.
17. Robert Graves: *The White Goddess,* Faber & Faber, 1961, p. 127.
18. C. Kerenyi: *The Gods of the Greeks.* Thames & Hudson, 1951, p. 28.
19. Erich Neumann: *The Great Mother,* Bollingen Series, Princeton University Press, 1972 edn, p. 267.
20. S. H. Langdon: *Mythology of All Races, Vol. 5: Semitic,* Cooper Square, 1964, p. 282.
21. Joseph Campbell, *The Masks of God: Occidental Mythology,* Souvenir Press, 1974, p. 7.
22. Langdon, op. cit., p. 102.
23. Athena, born from Zeus's head, appears to have been a local version of the Great Goddess, demoted by the spread of the patriarchal religion. See A. B. Cook, *Zeus* Vol. III, Cambridge University Press, 1940.
24. C. Kerenyi: *Zeus and Hera,* Chapter VII.
25. Esther Harding: *The Way of All Women,* Longmans, Green and Co., 1933, Chapter 2.

# 2.

# Astronomy

Next to the sun, Jupiter is the largest object in the solar system, more massive than all the other objects in the solar system combined, except for the sun itself, and 318 times as massive as the earth. Its diameter is 143,000km, about eleven times that of the earth. Despite its gigantic size, it is in fact composed mainly of light substances, gases, probably in the main hydrogen and helium. Beneath its clouds it has no solid surface. It radiates more energy than it receives from the sun, more than twice as much, at infra-red wavelengths. Some of the waves it emits burst out in storms of radio energy. It is thought that the asteroids known as Apollo objects, which intersect the earth's orbit and risk colliding with it, may in fact be produced by Jupiter. The Great Red Spot, seen on telescopes since 1831, may be a vast atmospheric vortex, a perpetual storm-system in the planet's atmosphere, bringing up red material from deeper levels. Jupiter spins faster than any other planet, but not entirely evenly, with an equatorial band moving faster than the rest. Its surface magnetic field is thought to be about ten times that of the earth, and is stronger than that of any other planet. Its gravitational pull is strong enough to affect the asteroid belt, and holds to the planet thirteen moons.

Principal source consulted: George O. Abell: *Realm of the Universe,* Holt, Rinehart & Winston, New York, 1976.

# 3.

# Jupiter and Saturn

We should pray as if everything depended on God, and act as if everything depended on ourselves.

St Augustine

It is clear from their interaction in mythology that Jupiter and Saturn, though related, represent forces which are inimical to each other. Their natures as described by astrology are so opposed that it is difficult, if not impossible, for them both to operate at the same time, yet they are complementary, the one requires the other. What goes up must come down, systole follows diastole and sowing leads to harvesting.

The two planets, which stand between the truly personal planets and the impersonal outer planets, make up a polarity whose terms might be variously translated as energy and matter, hope and fear, abundance and scarcity, expansion and contraction, or, in terms of Jung's functions, intuition and sensation.

The traditional labels of expansion and contraction are rather abstract, but acquire flesh if we relate them to our psychological experience in daily life, and the physical postures that correspond to them. Jupiter is that which encourages us to expand our lungs and reach out, promising that everything we need is within our grasp, or at least just around the corner. He fills us with a sense of boundless potential, whispering that all things are possible, inspiring and firing, leading us on, convincing us against all the odds. He gives us licence. He takes us out of ourselves.

But whereas Jupiterian trust opens us up, Saturnian fear makes us draw in, shrinks us, hunches our shoulders and bows our head, raises cynical doubts and mutters caution, censures and inhibits with feelings of inadequacy and painful self-consciousness. His advice is generally to play it safe and hang on to what we have. He is deeply suspicious of Jupiter's propensity for risk-taking. Kronos devoured the infant Zeus out of fear.

Saturn's security is Jupiter's prison. Saturn is the lord of boundaries, and Jupiter is not prepared to acknowledge any. He does not set out to destroy them, in the manner of the trans-Saturnian planets, by breaking through, dissolving or undermining them — he simply refuses to recognize that there are any limits, and indeed with his help mountains can be moved. But even in our most god-like moments, nemesis is waiting in the wings. Saturn reminds us that we are after all but flesh and blood, and we overstep our human limitations at our peril.

The limitations imposed by Saturn are ultimately those of the material world, for form necessarily implies definition, bounding, and for that matter binding. Saturn confines us to the real world, as experienced through the senses, and all our inspirations must ultimately stand the reality test or vanish into thin air.

Yet though we cannot in this life evade the fate of beings dwelling in a world of substance, the evidence of our senses is not the whole story — it would be a sad world if this were the case. The exact sciences weigh and measure and describe what we are accustomed to think of as external reality, but there is an inner mode of perception too, through the exercise of which we can see not what is under our nose, but what might be, what exists in potential. This is the vision of Jupiter, without which nothing new could come into being, we would have measurement devoid of meaning. Behind every man-made Saturnian structure lies an intuitive glimpse of its possibility. The successful business or institution was first conceived in imagination, and its material progress is dependent as much on the capacity to envision possible developments as on the regulation of material assets and the organization of time and motion.

Jupiter beckons and promises. He can deceive, like the Zeus of the myths, and he wears all sorts of disguises, but he points the way forward, and if we know how to recognize him, and also when it is time to turn and pay allegiance to Saturn and consolidate our understanding, we can go a long way towards fulfilling the promise.

Saturn and his sign are traditionally associated with the father, but Jupiter too, or Father Zeus, is also an aspect of the father principle.

In early childhood father — in the ideal situation — steps in to break up the originally symbiotic relationship between mother and child. He lays down limits on the child's behaviour which it is very difficult for mother to do, wrapped up in maternal closeness and identity with her offspring. This is the Saturnian aspect of fatherhood, much emphasized in the stern, censorious father of the Victorian novel.

But father has another function as well. He mediates the wide world outside the nursery where the fullness of life is promised, and a million possibilities await exploration. Perhaps I should add that the *roles* are interchangeable; the role of father may be carried by a woman, but in terms of human evolution the mothering role is something different, intimate and nurturing, concerned with immediate needs rather than the breadth of human experience. It is part of the role of the father to lead us out from the hearth and broaden our horizons. This is the function of Jupiter.

Jupiter is of course also Zeus the stud, progenitor, the fecundating principle, sower of seeds, and here contrasts again with Saturn, the god of the harvest with his sickle.

Father Zeus, laying down the law and hurling down thunderbolts can be as tyrannical as rigid Kronos, and whether we meet him in the family, at work or in politics it is possible to confuse the two. But the underlying motivation is very different, and the resulting style is also of a different order. Behind Saturn's rule-making lies fear and the need to play it safe and avoid risks and troublesome innovations. Nothing must be left to chance, nor must important decisions be left to the inexperienced or adventurous. Responsibility consists in not letting things or people get out of control.

The Jupiterian dictator on the other hand simply feels that he is right, and his word brooks no questioning, though it may represent but the whim of the moment. Defy him and he will at first draw himself up to his full height and pontificate or bluster, then fly into a rage, but he is unlikely to bear a grudge for long.

Another area where Jupiter and Saturn come into play is the dimension of time. It is generally considered that Saturn is the lord of time, but his domain is its limiting aspect: the constraints of the present situation, largely if not wholly dictated by our actions in the past (*karma*), and the awareness that our days are numbered. Saturn is conservative, and stresses the importance of learning the hard lessons of experience and doing things in ways that have proved effective. He is the old man looking back on life, suspicious of innovation.

Jupiter is associated with the gift of prophecy — which Zeus acquired by devouring Metis — and his realm is the world of possibilities, which always lies in the future — once a possibility has been given form it has entered Saturn's domain. But he also has a face turned towards the past. As the ruler of middle age he is also the man of experience, but here the word has a very different ring from its Saturnian use. Jupiter's concern is with the fullness of experience, the breadth of scope that comes with time. By mid-life we have many landmarks by which to orientate ourselves. We can dip into our experience to illustrate a point or find guidance or consolation, and enjoy the sense that we have come a long way. Alan Leo sees it this way:

> The sum total of our past is probably indicated by the planet Jupiter. Each individual is encircled by an aura, the boundary of which comes directly under the vibration of Jupiter. We expand and increase the size and quality of that aura during each earth life, and, whether in objective manifestation on the physical world or in the heaven, in the subjective worlds, this aura is our own and contains our whole history, the result of the past and the possibilities of the future . . .[1]

Emily Fawcus[2] has also pointed out that through his marriage to Mnemosyne, Zeus also has title to the rulership of memory. This is not the lunar memory of a cosy womb, but the intuition that our origin lies in divine brightness, that we come to this life 'trailing clouds of glory'.

As joint chronocrators or rulers of time, Jupiter and Saturn through their regular conjunctions recurring through the pattern of the triplicities, formed the measure of history long before the discovery of the outer planets. Jupiter's cycle (nearly twelve years) is comparable to the solar measure of the twelve-month year, while Saturn's cycle (two and a half years in each sign) relates to the lunar motion of two and a half days per sign. This alignment fits the masculine/ feminine elemental balance of the two planets, for Saturn though masculine in name belongs to the feminine element of earth.

To return to the complementary nature of the two planets with which this section began, there must be room in life both for faith and practical self-sufficiency, as Saint Augustine urged. The latter without the former is depressing and meaningless, but few can survive on faith alone, or change the world by virtue only of positive thinking.

Not only is cultivating the Jupiterian helpful to the individual weighed down by Saturn, but Saturn's restraint and form-giving power is also needed as counterweight to Jupiter's ungrounded enthusiasms. This is not usually welcome advice, however, for Jupiter flatters the ego, and Saturn does not.

## Notes

1. Alan Leo: *How to Judge a Nativity, Part I,* republished as *How to Judge a Nativity*, 'Astrology for All' Series, Fowler, London, 1969, pp. 35—6.
2. In the lecture given at the Astrological Association Conference at Exeter University, September 1984.

# 4.
# Jupiter and Mercury

As opposed to the four elements, which describe the composition
of the world we experience — the composition of the psyche if we
interpret the chart as a psychological map — the three qualities of
cardinal, fixed and mutable imply a sequence of beginning, middle
and end, or birth, life and death. Such a threefold sequence is to
be found in the triple-faced Moon Goddess (the maid, the mother,
the crone), the three Fates (Klotho who spins our life's thread, Lachesis
who measures it, Atropos the inflexible who cuts it off), and the
Indian *Trimurti* (Brahma the Creator, Vishnu the Preserver and Shiva
the Destroyer).

There is confirmation of this idea in Edward Edinger's discussion
of the trinity archetype,[1] in which he also contrasts this simple
threefold progression through time with the threefold format of
thesis, antithesis and synthesis. The term 'common' as an alternative
to 'mutable', suggesting that these signs combine the qualities of
cardinal and fixed, would fit the succession of quadruplicities into
this second pattern.

The cardinal signs are dynamic and get things moving; one can
look at them perhaps as motivating forces. The fixed signs hold,
maintain, resist change like attitudes which have been formed and
are not up for questioning. The mutable signs involve letting go,
scattering, distributing, dispersing the energy stored in the fixed
signs. They do not cling, but go the way the wind blows, and thus
are always on the move. If we relate these qualities to the stages of
life, the mutable stage corresponds to loosening one's hold on the
world, allowing what one has stored to be redistributed, seeing the
relativity of what one has created and held onto in the past.

The three mutable signs may be considered as aspects of what we call mind[2] (granted that this is a loose term, and that it may also be used to embrace all astrological phenomena): Gemini the conceptualizing mind, Virgo the practical mind, or thought integrated with matter, Sagittarius the exploring and visionary mind and Pisces the ego-transcending, meditative mind. While the two Mercurial signs understand experience in terms of distinctions and facts, the Jupiterian signs are often more at home with intuitive perceptions, images and symbolism. I am not comfortable with the label 'higher mind' which is sometimes attached to Jupiter, as this leaves to Mercury the 'lower mind' and seems to imply some sort of relative value. Each of the planets is surely to be seen as an essential part of a working whole. It may be argued, however, that Mercury represents a more fundamental process. We experience the cycle of Mercury in little more than our first year of life, whereas we are practically adolescent by the time Jupiter has circled the horoscope. Correspondingly, we learn language and the basic co-ordination of our limbs before we are ready for philosophical flights or for setting off for distant places.

Mercury, at his purest in Gemini, likes to work in a binary fashion: 'if it is not this it must be that', proceeding by a logical forking process. He also represents the principle of exchange: 'this *for* that'. Virgo, for practical purposes, separates out the sheep from the goats. The following passage seems to me to speak of Mercury: 'Indeed, to some extent, it has always been necessary and proper for a man, in his thinking, to divide things up and to separate them, so as to reduce his problems to manageable proportions; for evidently, if in our practical technical work we tried to deal with the whole of reality at once, we would be swamped'.[3] Mercury enables us to make sense of things, to 'grasp' them with our minds by making distinctions and, conversely, by making connections between one thing and another. Such was the gain from biting the fruit of the tree of knowledge. But with Mercury and no Jupiter we might lose sight of the greater whole.

A good example of the Mercurial process is the classificatory system of Linnaeus by means of which all members of the animal and vegetable kingdoms are distinguished. It should come as no surprise that Linnaeus was born when the Sun was in Gemini. Gemini seems to enjoy the sheer multiplicity of phenomena, and giving names to them. The 'practical technical work' mentioned above is the Virgoan application of the same principle. But that aspect of mind

which differentiates and connects and proceeds in logical steps can
be tricky, as lovers of paradoxes and conundrums will know. It can
prove to us that the fleet-footed Achilles can never catch up with
the tortoise. Mercury can lead us delightfully up the (forking) garden
path. He is adept at sleights of hand and a master of disguises.

Jupiter (like courting Zeus) can also be roguish and also change
his shape. With the mutables generally nothing is stable: now you
see it, now you don't. Sagittarius is here today and gone tomorrow,
Pisces constantly changes form and colour. The new co-ruler of Pisces,
Neptune, stands in for numerous shape-shifting sea gods and
goddesses such as Nereus, Proteus, Metis and Thetis, but Jupiter
too can be slippery and is far from being a reliable planet. On the
one hand he can bluff, on the other he lapses into gullibility.

Jupiter's approach to understanding is not analytical. He seeks
underlying laws and purposes and is willing to make intuitive leaps.
Taking things apart is alien to him. This is why he is said to be
debilitated in Mercury's signs. If for Mercury two and two make four,
or occasionally five, Jupiter has an affinity with the Pythagorean
approach to numbers: it is the elusive element of meaning he is
looking for rather than an accounting system.

Jupiter and his signs are not intrinsically orderly, and lack the
precision in which the Mercurial signs excel. Jupiter's signs can be
careless, untidy, even abandoned. They often don't know when to
stop, and have a rather cavalier attitude to facts. Jupiter takes a broad
view of things, lapses into sweeping generalizations and is impatient
with detail. He is not so much concerned with particulars as with
seeking out the underlying principles which will set immediate
problems in a broader framework, be it religious, philosophical, or
even scientific. He is inclined to substitute faith for Mercury's more
sceptical approach. He is focused on something beyond the present
situation, and that something can be quite intoxicating. If Mercury,
god of crossroads, is involved with immediate decisions about which
way to turn, Jupiter is concerned with the journey itself and the
possibilities it holds in store. He is the planet of the way, of the
meandering path.

Mercury is often considered to govern thinking, but this is not
a simple equation. If by thinking we mean processing of ideas and
information, that indeed is Mercury's function. Jupiter, however,
comes into the picture too, as *the capacity to look beyond what is
given,* the ability, we might say, to *think speculatively* or creatively.

This is not necessarily an intellectual process, but it is a ninth house issue. The university student who cannot in some way go beyond what has been taught and explore the subject independently may get a degree, but has not really left the schoolroom of the third house.

This aspect of Jupiter's function is well illustrated by David Hamblin's experiment with groups of students, reported on in the *Astrological Journal*.[4] Teaching students in classes with high proportions of births with Jupiter in the same sign he set them as a group task an organizational design exercise, and found that the results correlated strongly with the dominant Jupiter sign. The same tendency was shown in group discussion exercises. Unfortunately he was only able to run the exercise with groups dominated by six Jupiter signs. Of course the Jupiter-in-Leo and Jupiter-in-Gemini did best. The former made splendid presentations, utilizing to the full the opportunity to display their academic flair in front of their fellow students. The latter group were in their element; an exercise in which they were to explore possibilities through exchange of ideas might have been designed with them in mind. The Jupiter-in-Cancer group, which would probably have preferred to dream up their projects in private, came off worst. The Jupiter-in-Libra group used the opportunity to explore their own interpersonal relationships rather than the task in hand, while in the Jupiter-in-Scorpio group some worked with great determination while others showed little interest. No doubt it would have been more appropriate in this case too to set tasks for lone deliberation. The Jupiter-in-Sagittarius group were entertaining, but too undisciplined to do really well. A Jupiter-in-Virgo group did not do the task, but took quite well to group discussion and made a name for themselves by being particularly critical of the course, which proved constructive.

The mutable signs, with the possible exception of Pisces, are connected not only with learning but also with teaching. (Arguably, Pisces teaches on a more subtle level, or perhaps 'mediates' would be a more appropriate verb.) Dissemination, the scattering of seeds of knowledge and understanding, is an aspect of mutability, and both Mercury and Jupiter manifest as teacher and as guide, Mercury informing and making connections, Jupiter inspiring the student to seek. Indeed, he is known as the 'guru' in the Hindu tradition.[5] With the Mercurical teacher we need to be on our guard against being led astray by the 'facts', but with the Jupiterian teacher we must be aware of the dangers of enthusiasm — a slightly suspect virtue. I know several people who were so enthused by a marvellously Jupiterian religious teacher that they speedily became monks and nuns. When the teacher left, however, they wondered what on earth they had done and soon set about taking off their robes and sorting out their confusion.

Before leaving this section on the rulers of the mutables, I would like to underline the fact that Jupiter's rulership of exclusively mutable signs is no accident. We may love him, but he is not nearly as constant as we would like him to be. Like the vision that fades, like the restless mind, like the teacher who inspires and departs he is always moving on.

## Notes

1.   Edward Edinger: *Ego and Archetype,* Putnam, New York, 1972, Chapter 7.
2.   This is the idea of Zipporah Dobyns in *Finding the Person in the Horoscope,* T.I.A. Publications, 1973.
3.   David Bohm: *Wholeness and the Implicate Order,* Routledge & Kegan Paul, 1981 edn, p.2 (First pubd 1980).
4.   David Hamblin: 'Jupiter in the Classroom', *Astrological Journal,* issued by the Astrological Association of Great Britain, Summer 1978 and Summer 1981.
5.   Chris Eger: 'Swami Muktananda', *Astrological Journal,* autumn 1982.

# 5.
# Elements

The element traditionally associated with Jupiter is air. This may come as a surprise to some readers, as our planet enjoys no special connection with any of the airy signs, and through his undisputed rulership of Sagittarius might be thought to be most at home in the fiery triplicity, perhaps, as ruler of Pisces, also having a watery side. But the association of elements with planets is not derived from the signs they rule, as is sometimes assumed. The identification of triplicities, that is to say of *signs*, with elements appears to be of relatively recent date. Though Ptolemy refers to triplicities, or 'trigons', composed of signs of harmonious (trine) relationship with each other, I have so far found no reference to the triplicities as being fiery, earthy and so forth pre-dating the seventeenth century. On the other hand, the association of *planets* with the four elements was current in the Middle Ages and Renaissance, and adapted to astrology the system of the four temperaments which arose from the Hippocratic and Galenic tradition of medicine. It is worth a little exploration to get a sense of what the elements have meant to our forebears and to understand why Jupiter was considered an airy planet.

The elements, individually and grouped together, were for a millennia the object of veneration and later of cosmological speculation, as well as providing a fruitful source of metaphor. At the mythological level, history was often thought to have originated with the divine marriage between sky god (Uranus) and earth goddess (Gaia), and there were myths about great watery deities, such as Okeanos and Tethys. In the classical pantheon, Zeus ruled the sky, Poseidon the waters, and Hades the depths of the earth. The Sumerians had a trilogy of Anu (representing the sky), Enlil (earth) and Ea (water). Then there were gods connected with fire. Marduk

was one, Hephaestos, god of volcanoes, the Titan Prometheus who
brought fire to humanity, and of course the Iranian Ahura Mazda.
These gods were not simply deifications of the physical elements,
but of life principles which those elements seemed to embody.

By the sixth century BC a more scientific mood was developing.
The pre-Socratic Greek philosophers were concerned with defining
the nature of the physical universe, but the earlier mythological
connotations echo through their theories, and they appear to have
viewed the elements with something like religious awe. The elements
emerge from the fragments of pre-Socratic writings as powerful images
as well as tangible substances. Goethe develops this theme in *Faust*,
Part Two, where he includes a debate on the relative power of water
and fire between the philosophers Thales and Anaxagoras.[1] Goethe
is clearly on the side of non-violent water, and Anaxagoras soon
disappears from the scene. Not surprisingly, Goethe's own horoscope
has five planets and the ascendant in water signs, and a watery grand
trine, at one corner of which is Jupiter in Pisces.

The notion that the cosmos was made up of *four* elements was
current among the Pythagoreans, but it is generally claimed that
the charismatic fifth-century BC philosopher Empedocles first
described *man* as being composed of these same four cosmic
elements, or four *roots* as he called them, which he also linked with
the earth, the sky, the sun and the sea.[2] The stoics, who
enthusiastically took up astrology, also adhered to the Empedoclean
model, though without incorporating the four elements into their
astrological system.[3] What links connect the Western tradition with
the similar Indian schema[4] is not clear. In the West the four elements
were in due course paired with the four temperaments of humoral
medicine, following Hippocrates and Galen. These were the sanguine
(airy), choleric (fiery), phlegmatic (watery) and melancholic (earthy)
temperaments.

Let us look a little more closely at the individual elements and
their associations.

## Earth

In starting with earth I start with the obvious. It is Dr Johnson who,
outraged at Bishop Berkeley's proof of the non-existence of matter,
'striking his foot with mighty force against a large stone, till he
rebounded from it, answered, "I refute it *thus*." '[5] It is the Buddha
in his traditional earth-touching gesture, calling the earth to witness

the reality of his enlightenment. As James Hillman has pointed out, if individuals lack air we do not send them up in an aeroplane, but if they lack earth we suggest they get out a spade and dig the soil. Earth implies a literal-mindedness, taking things on the obvious level, the level which in the minds of many people constitutes incontrovertible reality. Perhaps it was by virtue of its very matter-of-factness that though early philosophers were to be found claiming supremacy for water (Thales), air (Anaximenes) and fire (Heraclitus), none gives pride of place to boring, solid earth. It remained for the alchemists to take solid matter as their primary metaphor, starting with the *prima materia* and ending with the philosophers' stone. The early philosophers seem to have started at the other end, seeking to explain the solid in terms of some higher principle.

Earth may on one level represent the obvious, the banal, but it is also the mysterious mother of all physical being, the dust we come from and go to, and the source of all fruitfulness, productivity and wealth. Earth is the element most persistently identified with the Goddess, as mistress of material welfare and lady of the granaries, green, golden, opulent. It was easy, when the time came, to identify as earth signs half of those already characterized as feminine. (The positive/negative polarity of signs was an ancient distinction.)

Earth also implies the unavoidable limitations of physical existence, representing the curse of birth into the physical body often despised by those with transcendental aspirations and thus chronically undervalued in the Christian tradition, which follows Aristotle's spirit/matter split. It is matter, substance, (animal) nature, to be worked, subdued, refined. It can be measured and organized, and used to build solid structures. Saturn came to be associated with this humble element, which was placed at the bottom of Aristotle's vertical schema,[6] with water, air and (topmost) fire above it. The same vertical order is also to be found in the Kabbalistic system.[7] Good, reliable earth, the bottom line, beast of burden, provider of goods, which when overvalued leads to materialism, when undervalued becomes dreary necessity and imprisoning flesh.

## Water

Thales of Miletus, in the sixth century BC, held that the earth floated on water and probably that everything originated from it. In this it seems likely that he had had contact with Babylonian thought, which put the watery deities Apsu and Tiamat at the beginning of

all things. In the story of Eridu, Marduk is said to have built a raft
on the primeval waters, and a hut on the raft which became the
earth,[8] while in the Babylonian Creation Epic Marduk creates heaven
and earth from the watery body of Tiamat.[9] A similar origin is hinted
at occasionally in the Bible too. For example Psalm 136 tells us that
God 'stretched out the earth above the waters', while the Koran says
that water is the origin of all life. Homer in passing (*Iliad*, Book XIV)
mentions Okeanos and Tethys as the original divine parents. This
image of the earth, or life, emerging from the waters, which can
be related to the emergence of life from the sea, of the baby from
the watery womb, of islands of consciousness from the sea of the
unconscious, seems to refer back to a dimly remembered past where
there was no separateness, and fits easily with the water signs of the
zodiac, perhaps most of all with the Moon's sign, Cancer. And the
place we come from may be the place to which we return, like droplets
merging again with the ocean. The symbolism of baptism is that
of rebirth from a new womb, and of cleansing, for water both refreshes
and washes us clean.

One of the best-known quotations from Heraclitus is the one which
uses the image of the river into which we cannot step twice.[10] Water
is the element which most readily puts us in mind of impermanence,
change, flux, instability. Its essence seems better described by verbs
than by adjectives or nouns: flowing, surging, merging, dissolving,
sprinkling. It is sensitive to the slightest movement. Essentially chaotic
and lacking inherent form it was regarded with some disfavour by
the orderly Confucius, whose genius lay in perceiving and prescribing
structure, and its want of definition or self-set limitation connects
it with states of confusion and psychosis. It may appear clear, but
it can be deceptive. Its reflected images are, from earth's point of
view, illusory. To Lao Tzu, the mystical poet and philosopher of Taoism,
however, 'Highest good is like water'[11] because it is non-contentious
and settles in the lowest spots, follows the path of least resistance,
flows effortlessly into every available space and makes itself at home.
Arguably, water rather than earth should be considered the lowest
element as it so well illustrates the principle of depth, and sea-level
is the bottom line from which we measure all geographical height.
Though there are male water deities, water and moisture have most
often been associated with the feminine;[12] Lao Tzu's high estimation
of water goes with a philosophy which advises us to 'keep to the role
of the female'.[13] Water shares with earth, which also moves

downwards, the feminine, yin or negative signs of the zodiac. Traditionally it has been associated with the Moon, or with Venus.

## Fire

The non-gravitational elements, those associated with the sky and its fires, have generally been allotted to the masculine. The sexism of superior and inferior, a distinction derived from a value system which prefers what is above (the masculine) to what is below (the feminine), and judges height as more desirable than depth, has on the whole conferred greater value on the elements of fire and air.

Most descriptions of astrological fire stress its heating and burning power: ardour, passion, excitability. The fiery type became the choleric, described by Nicholas Culpeper, the seventeenth-century herbalist and medical astrologer, as 'bold, unashamefac'd, furious, hasty, quarrelsom, irefull . . . courageous, gracelesse . . .'.[14] Fire, however, does not only heat, burn, consume. It is also light, a fact which we in the age of electric light can be excused for forgetting. What Culpeper is describing I would associate with Mars, the red planet, rather than with fire in general. Galen, on whose theories the system of temperaments is built, had held a different and less Martian view of the choleric type: it enjoyed 'acuteness and intelligence of the mind'.[15]

Mythology also makes clear that there are two kinds of fire, though the distinction is not necessarily identical with that made above. There is the fire associated with gods of the sky and its illuminations, the fire, presumably that Prometheus stole atop Mount Olympus, and the fire that issues, sometimes with devastating results, from below the earth, from the realm of Hephaestos. Though a useful god, who at his hot anvil produced the weapons and attributes of the Olympian pantheon, Hephaestos was not the kind of deity one could imagine becoming a ruler among gods. Mars, whom we consider the fiery planet *par excellence,* was, you may remember, the exclusive product of his mother Hera, spouse of Zeus and earlier an independent goddess. He was conceived without masculine help out of revenge against Zeus for his unnatural act in giving birth to Athena from his head. Mars thus comes from the outraged feminine, his fire is not the fire of heaven.

By Culpeper's day, the fiery temperament had become identified largely with the more macho characteristics of the element, anything but spiritual. This was certainly not what the Stoics had in mind in giving fire the most elevated position on their scale.

When Heraclitus described fire as the basic stuff the world is made of, he meant 'the purest and brightest sort, that is, as of the aitherial and divine thunderbolt'.[16] There had long been a tradition that held *aither*, the fiery substance deemed to brighten the sky, in especial reverence, and it was often supposed that this divine, heavenly fire was also the stuff souls were made of. The Babylonians also held that souls were of the same fiery essence as the stars.[17] Consider a corpse. It is cold because the fiery soul, the spark of life, has left it. On death, the soul was often considered to return to its bright heavenly home. It seems to me that in some way Prometheus' theft of fire is connected with his role as creator of mankind — he had the power to animate, to create life and soul. His gift of power to men could be construed as giving them, too, creative powers. Yahweh, who lives in heaven and also created man, also appears from time to time in the form of fire. He speaks from the burning bush (Ex. iii. 2,3) and descends as fire from heaven to consume his dedicatory sacrifice in the new temple (2 Chron. vii. 1). Astrologically, fire is strongly connected with the creative urge.

Heraclitus' thunderbolt, of course, is also the attribute of Zeus. It is fire from heaven, the expression of the wrath of God. It is obviously as fire that Zeus reveals himself to Semele who, egged on by vengeful Hera, asks him to reveal himself to her in his true form, whereupon she is reduced to ashes. It seems to me that Jupiter in fact has strong fiery associations. His Greek name signifies brightness, his Babylonian equivalent is often called a fire god.[18] Mars, the Sun and Jupiter can all be considered fiery planets, the latter two having qualities of light as well as heat. Light is also a metaphor for consciousness, which Jupiter, like the Sun, strives for.

Fire is the element that most nearly corresponds to our notion of energy, whether we experience it as pulsing physical force and animal spirits or divine creative principle, and indeed there is no reason to consider these as ultimately different in nature.

### Air
Air is again associated with the principle of height, and astrologically with looking down on things from above, detached (in contrast to the involvement of water), seeing things in perspective, with clarity and sharpness. It enables a broad overview, which is certainly consistent with the meaning of Jupiter. From detachment comes

the possibility of abstract thought and the purity of ideas.

When Anaximenes declared that air was infinite and divine, and was the principle from which all things came into being 'it seems that [he] regarded air as the breath of the world'.[19] As was the case with fire, an ancient tradition associated air or breath with soul, the invisible element that gives life to what without animation would be mere solid and fluid matter. This view was embedded in the Greek and Latin languages, where *pneuma* (spirit), *psyche* (soul) and *anima* (soul) all originally meant breath. *Pneuma* is also the word used for the Holy Spirit, which descended (presumably from heaven) as an airborne creature, a dove. For the ancients it held similar connotations to the Sanskrit *prana* and the Chinese *chi,* the life-giving and life-enhancing energy that enters the body with the breath. Prometheus in fact *breathes* life into his dust-men. The soul used sometimes to be depicted as a butterfly leaving the lips of a dying person. Breath on the global level is wind — the fertilizing wind of Jupiter? It cannot be denied that the Jupiterian temperament is often distinctly breezy.

Now Galen attributed to the sanguine or airy type 'simplicity bordering on foolishness',[20] but this view did not hold ground for long. Whereas fire as a determining factor in temperament acquired grosser characteristics, the airy temperament drew to itself all the superior qualities. Writing in the twelfth century, William of Conches identified air as the element proper to man, that which raised him above the beasts, who consisted only of the other three.[21] Animals presumably breathed in those days, but were not held to have souls. Human beings, originally created all with the blessed sanguine temperament, enjoyed a distinction identified with that same substance of which Anaximenes had held the gods were made. The identification of air with that which is specifically human is again reflected in the images of the air signs, human figures rather than animals in two cases, a human artefact in the third. That the majority of people suffered from temperaments other than sanguine was for William of Conches a consequence of mankind's degeneracy. The sanguine person, good-natured, good-looking, cheerful and nearer to God, was the individual associated with the Great Benefic.

A partial explanation for the exaltation of the airy type lies in the nature of the four humours or bodily fluids as defined in the Hippocratic writings. While yellow bile, black bile and phlegm were considered 'superflous humours', blood occupied a rather special position as an obviously vital substance. Hippocrates had already tentatively linked physical characteristics to the psychological and moral realm,[22] but Galen, in the second century AD 'emphasised more clearly than anyone else the direct causal connexion between bodily constitution and character'.[23] Out of Galen's work developed the system of the temperaments (*krases,* or mixtures), which constituted both physical and psychological types. The temperaments were, in the early centuries of the Christian era, likened to, or said to imitate, the elements, and blood in this system was matched with air. In each temperament a particular humour was held to predominate, although the balance of humours in an individual would vary from time to time, leading through imbalance to sickness, and each humour was considered to gain ascendancy during one of the four seasons. The four elements had already formed a relationship with the 'qualities' of hot, cold, moist and dry, a tetrad first defined by Empedocles' successor Philistion (Fig. 1). By Galen's day the humours already bore the relationship to the qualities and

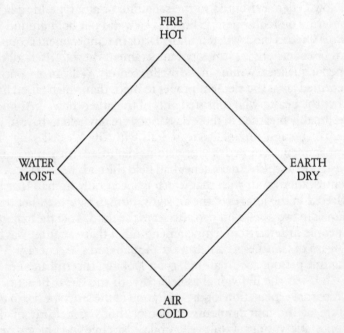

*Fig. 1*   The Four Elements and the Four Qualities in the relationship defined by Philistion.

seasons presented in Fig. 2, and elements were soon added in,[24] followed later by planets. Over the centuries, Galen's system came back to Europe with the Arabs, who had adopted it. There were variations on this map, with different planets allocated to the elements in some cases, but this is the schema that eventually prevailed. The planets are characterized in this fashion by William Lilly in the seventeenth century.

It is interesting to note that just as fire and air vied with each other for pride of place, so there was later confusion between the earthy and watery types 'so that in the fifteenth- and sixteenth-century illustrations the portrait of the melancholic frequently changed places with the portrait of the phlegmatic, sometimes one and sometimes the other occupying the third place, whereas the sanguine regularly appeared first and the choleric second'.[25] The line separating the

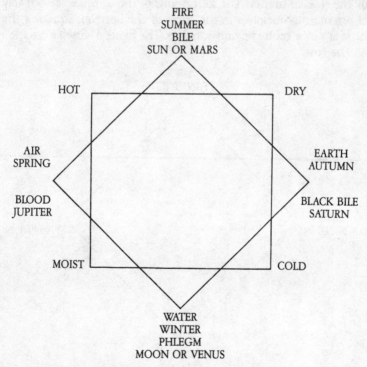

*Fig. 2* The Humours and Seasons in relationship to the Qualities established in the *Corpus Hippocraticum* (fifth century B.C.), with the Elements and Planets later attributed to them.

'masculine' from the 'feminine' elements, however, was never blurred.

The principle of 'fourness' dates at least from the Pythagoreans, who held the number four in especial reverence. The four elements have parallels in the four suits of the Tarot, the four evangelists and their beasts, and Jung's four functions of consciousness. The list could of course be extended considerably. As Figs. 1 and 2 illustrate, four is the number on which the mandala is based, and forms a figure with two pairs of opposites. It is sometimes considered as signifying completeness, and Plato said: 'The quaternary is the number connected with the *realization* of the idea' (the number three representing the idea itself). Agreeing with Plato, modern astrologers have seen in the fourth harmonic and the square aspect the principle of *manifestation*. [26] As such, four is the number of earth, represented by the cross of matter. The four points of the compass are our way of orientating ourselves in the circle of the horizon, squaring the circle at whose centre we find ourselves. The figure 4 is itself a variation on the cross.

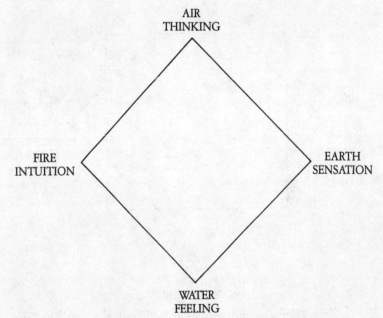

*Fig. 3* The Four Elements in relation to the Jungian Functions of Consciousness (Liz Greene).

The Indian schema places ether at the centre point of the four elements, as the alchemists did with their *quint*essence. The Chinese have five elements, splitting earth into metal and wood, but again these are often depicted in the form of a mandala. There is clearly something very satisfying and stable about such four-sided figures.

Liz Greene, drawing an analogy between Jung's four functions of consciousness (thinking, feeling, sensation, intuition) and the four elements (air, water, earth, fire, respectively) presents us with an alternative map (Fig. 3). This is also a valuable contribution, throwing more light on the nature of the elements and the way they interact, the opposites in this case being even more opposed in nature than those on the traditional map. I do not feel that any of these diagrams is definitive. The traditional map has its weaknesses, particularly in the linkage between elements and qualities which results in the nature of air corresponding to *warm and moist.* Whatever the climate where the map was devised, it is hard to understand why the nature of air should be considered *essentially* warm and moist — unless air is seen as an extension of breath. The connection between air and the thinking function may also provide an explanation for its overvaluation in our Western tradition, for thinking has certainly been favoured since Socrates, though we have moved from an earlier intuitive thinking to a more scientific sensation-thinking, which would correspond with a shift from air/fire to air/earth.

From his place on the traditional map, Jupiter is linked with spring, the season of *growth,* the season of Marduk's festival, and in Chaucer's words the time when 'longen folk to goon on pilgrimages'[27] which are doubly ninth house affairs. By opposition Jupiter is connected with Saturn, so that Saturn's loss as representative of despised earth is Jupiter's gain. The Great Benefic balances the Great Malefic, the one overvalued as the other has been undervalued (though Saturn compensated by acquiring a special status of his own[28]). Cultivating the Jupiterian qualities was considered an antidote to Saturn-induced melancholy. We might, for example, send someone suffering from depression on a journey to rekindle his/her interest in the world.

Regarding Jupiter's proper element, I feel, for the reasons I have outlined, that he certainly has a claim to being considered fiery, as well as airy. His nature is of the two 'superior' elements. He generally blends well with the watery, too, as is evidenced by his rulership of Pisces and his exaltation in Cancer. The sensitivity of the water signs softens Jupiter's sometimes tyrannical nature. It is the Piscean side

of Jupiter that I sense in the Kabbalistic association of the planet
with mercy.[29] But weighed down by earth he is least at home and
has more of a struggle. As Socrates says in Plato's *Phaedo*, '[The true
philosopher] would like, as far as he can, to get away from the body',
and Jupiter, the planet of philosophy, high places and the far reaches
of human understanding is not particularly at home in the physical
realm. Nor are either of the signs he rules.

## Notes

1.  J. W. Goethe: *Faust/Part Two*, trans. Philip Wayne, Penguin,
    1959, pp. 134—6.
2.  R. Klibansky, E. Panofsky and F. Saxl: *Saturn and Melancholy*,
    Nelson, 1964, Chapter 1. I was greatly assisted in writing this
    chapter by this monumental work of scholarship.
3.  See Manilius: *Astronomica*, G. P. Goold, Harvard University Press
    and Heinemann (Loeb Classical Texts), 1977. He refers specifically
    to the doctrine of elements in a section on cosmological theory,
    but does not mention elements in connection with astrological
    symbolism.
4.  For more detailed discussion of the Indian system see S. Arroyo:
    *Astrology, Psychology and the Four Elements*, CRCS, 1975.
5.  Boswell's *Life of Johnson*, 6 Aug. 1763.
6.  See Manilius: op. cit.
7.  See Warren Kenton: *The Antomy of Fate: Kabbalistic Astrology*,
    Rider, 1978.
8.  G. S. Kirk, J. E. Raven and M. Schofield: *The Presocratic
    Philosophers*, Cambridge University Press, 1983 (2nd edn), p. 92.
9.  S. H. Langdon: *Mythology of All Races, Vol. 5: Semitic*, Cooper
    Square Pubs., New York, 1964, p. 282.
10. See Kirk, Raven and Schofield, op. cit. p. 195.
11. Lao Tzu: *Tao Te Ching*, trans. D. C. Lau, Penguin, 1963, p. 64.
12. A. Bouche-Leclercq in *L'Astrologie Grecque*, Paris, 1899, p. 91,
    says: 'C'était une opinion commune chez les 'physiciens' [the
    pre-Socratic philosophers] que l'énergie masculine était analogue
    à celle de la chaleur, tandis que la fonction feminine avait des
    affinités étroites avec le principe humide.'
13. Lao Tzu: *Tao Te Ching*, p. 85.
14. N. Culpeper: *Astrological Judgement of Disease*, London, 1655,
    p. 141.
15. Quoted in Klibansky, Panofsky and Saxl: *Saturn and Melancholy*,
    p. 58.

16. Kirk, Raven and Schofield, op. cit, p. 198.
17. F. V. M. Cumont: *Astrology and Religion among the Greeks and Romans,* Putnam, New York, 1912, p. 34.
18. S. H. Langdon: *Mythology of All Races, Vol. 5: Semitic,* Cooper Square Pubs., New York, 1964, p. 156.
19. Kirk, Raven and Schofield, op. cit, p. 147.
20. *Saturn and Melancholy,* p. 58.
21. Ibid. p. 102ff.
22. Ibid. p. 55.
23. Ibid. p. 57.
24. Ibid. p. 58.
25. Ibid. p. 64.
26. For example, David Hamblin in *Harmonic Charts,* Aquarian, 1983, p. 36.
27. G. Chaucer: *Canterbury Tales,* General Prologue, line 12.
28. This is the theme of *Saturn and Melancholy.*
29. See Warren Kenton: *The Anatomy of Fate,* Rider, 1978.

# 6.
# Travel

From the spiritual point of view, the journey is never merely a passage through space, but rather an expression of the urgent desire for discovery and change that underlies the actual movement and experience of travelling. Hence, to study, to inquire, to seek or to live with intensity through new and profound experiences are all modes of travelling or, to put it another way, spiritual and symbolic equivalents of the journey . . . Travelling, Jung observes, is an image of aspiration, of an unsatisfied longing that never finds its goal, seek where it may. [1]

Through his association with the ninth house, Jupiter is the lord of travel and all things foreign. The itchy feet of many an individual with a strong Jupiter keep him or her quite literally on the move, while for others the same restlessness operates inwardly. For all those with an emphasis on Jupiter, Sagittarius or the ninth house the myth of the journey has a particular relevance, and Thursday's child (born on Thor's or Jupiter's day) has far to go. Travel ideally *broadens* the mind, enables us to see things in a wider context. Jupiter rules the horse, which enabled us to extend the possibilities of travel, and presumably has connections with the train (iron horse) and the motor-car, too.

The urge to seek and explore is a powerful one, and is inseparable from a degree of dissatisfaction with what is known and familiar. There is a divine discontent that whispers in the Jupiterian ear, 'there must be more to life than this'; satisfaction leads to contentment and stasis, which is anathema to Jupiter. Whether travelling in the intellect, in spirit, in the world of the senses or the realm of the emotions, the enemy he most fears is boredom. The Sagittarian, like the Athenians whom Saint Paul railed at, often spends his time 'in nothing else but either to tell or to hear some new thing'. If the situation stagnates, he must pump new life and meaning into it, or else bid goodbye and move quickly on.

The 'mover on' is a familiar version of the traveller. Ever eager for fresh experience, he sets off again; yesterday's events fading already, slip into their places in his mind to add to the wealth of life's experience, contributing little to the weight of his pack. For him the farthest field always has a compelling greenness, a destination always beckons, a provisional one at any rate. Usually less conscious is the desire to leave something behind, to avoid the conflicts that result from involvement, from settling down: the compromises with partners and neighbours, the battle to retain an individual purpose amid responsibility for dependants with their own sense of direction — the prospect of such ties may terrify the traveller, and for his freedom from these complications he lightly sacrifices comparative security. He has something of the eternal adolescent about him, preferring to sample the sweetness of life and pass on before the promise fades. No obligations, no regrets. This is the youthful face of Jupiter, who mocks the stern father-figure of Saturn and is easily granted the indulgence of successive mother-figures, dismaying or infuriating those who attempt to tie him down. Like the freewheeling Bob Dylan (Sagittarius rising, Sun conjunct Jupiter and Uranus), who moved on musically to the outrage of many of his fans, he tosses over his shoulder the parting words: 'Don't think twice, it's all right'. His relationships are fun while they last.

Rootlessness is not always without regret, however. 'I have no home, no country, no family,' said Isabelle Eberhardt, a compulsive wanderer, 'I have lived all my life as a stranger.' The lack of a sense of belonging can hit the eternal drifter unexpectedly or creep up on him unawares. And when the meaning goes out of it, travel has its own particular brand of futility: 'The further one goes/The less one knows.'[2] It can even become a punishment. The Ancient Mariner, the Flying Dutchman, the Wandering Jew present images of a journey which is tyranny rather than freedom: the traveller who can't stop, his only hope a divine intervention of some kind.

The traveller is hard-pressed to survive without the more settled communities through which he passes, for the people whose bread he eats and for whom he occasionally betrays a hint of contempt.

They may play Hera to his Zeus. But he can give as well as take, and herein lies his welcome. He brings at the very least stories of exotic places and colourful adventures to awaken the imagination of those he meets, and in some stories he brings a kind of redemption, the stranger who walks in and saves the situation. Superman and the Lone Ranger are modern versions of the eternal traveller, unable to return home and with but a distant destination, sufficient to keep him on the move. On his way he enters into the affairs of those he drops in on and, like Santa Claus, leaves them better off than he found them. A hitch-hiker is welcome if he can relieve the boredom of the motorway, and doubly so if he is able to fix a sick engine. Knights errant are expected to perform deeds of valour as they pass, their social contribution. Ahasuerus, the hapless wandering Jew, performs invaluable services for his hosts. Nor is the mention of Father Christmas frivolous, for he combines the theme of travelling with the Sagittarian virtue of generosity. It is apt that Saint Nicholas, the original Santa Claus, has his feast day on the sixth of December, in the Sagittarian month.

Though we must have a destination, we are travellers only so long as we do not arrive. The joy of the true traveller is the journey itself. The poet Charles Baudelaire (Jupiter conjunct Sun and square Uranus — see below for relevance of Jupiter/Uranus contacts) describes the end of a voyage: the other passengers say 'At last!', but he sighs 'Already!' The great nineteenth-century Alexandrian poet Cavafy (Jupiter trine Uranus, birth time unknown) offers the following advice to that most hardened of travellers, Odysseus, whom he encourages to make the most of the places he passes through:

Always keep Ithaca in mind
To reach there is your destiny;
But never hurry — better if
You travel on for many years
To moor at last a grey-haired man,
Rich with your gatherings on the way,
No more expecting wealth from Ithaca. [3]

Transits to Jupiter and through the ninth frequently manifest as journeys. I made my own first trip abroad (notice how Jovian the word *abroad* is) when Jupiter entered my ninth house for the first time, and vividly recall the sense of wonder and discovery. Almost every moment there was some new experience, new tastes and smells, new kinds of people, new ways of doing things. To those with a strong Jupiterian emphasis such discoveries, and the freedom they give from the restrictions of routine, can be well-nigh addictive. Jupiter's house position too often indicates an area of restlessness and 'moving on', where an urge to explore accompanied by a desire for freedom militates against stagnation and constancy, and transits by Jupiter loosen us from our moorings and set us on the move again in the particular context indicated. The creative aspect of the travel motif is openness to new possibilities, the destructive, flight from commitment.

Looking at the charts of seasoned travellers printed in this chapter I have been struck by a common feature, namely major Jupiter/Uranus aspects, strongly emphasized by position and aspects to Sun and/or angles. The charts were selected purely because they

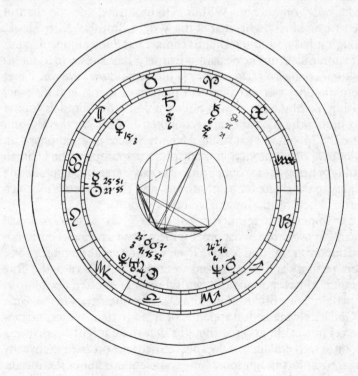

*Chart 1*
Moon Landing: 20 July, 1969, 8.17pm GMT.

belonged to enthusiastic travellers, and not on account of this factor, and yet it has come up every time. Even the poets mentioned — Baudelaire, Cavafy, Bob Dylan — whose journeys may have been more in imagination than reality — have strong Jupiter/Uranus contacts, and so does Isabelle Eberhardt, who is also mentioned above. Thomas Cook, father of the guided tour, is another exemplar. I have long noticed that these are about the most restless aspects going, those who have them in prominence being often unable to stay long in one home or job. Both planets place a high value on freedom, and put together they seem to signify a total impatience with restraint. A high proportion of astronauts also have these combinations, and the first landing of men on the moon was on the day of a Jupiter/Uranus conjunction (also conjunct the Moon!), marking a new era in travel possibilities. Similarly these aspects crop up in the charts of those involved in the early days of flight: Orville Wright had a wide conjunction, Wilbur Wright a trine, and the chart of the first manned flight, that of the Wright Brothers' Kitty Hawk, though it has no Jupiter/Uranus contact has Sun conjunct Uranus in Sagittarius. Antoine de Sainte-Exupery, best known to us for his children's book *The Little Prince* (a Jupiterian *puer aeternus* if ever there was one) was also an ardent pioneer of flying, and his other writings combine travel with philosophical reflection. His Jupiter is conjunct the IC and Uranus, opposed by Mars on the MC and trine the Moon and his ruling Mercury. There is an emphasis on innovative breakthrough in many of these examples, the Uranian quality of being ahead of one's time. There is also an uncompromising quality to the desire for new horizons, and this also tends to attach to the beliefs of the Jupiter/Uranus individual.

The nineteenth century saw the last great surge of colonial expansion by European nations. For them it was a period of optimism and opportunism. And hand in hand with the desire for more goods, more territory and new markets went the desire to carry the True Religion to new populations, with missionaries often doubling as imperial agents. Britain's lofty aim of destroying slavery in the name of God barely masked an appetite for access to trade routes and new sources of wealth, and the thought that there might be anything wrong in such exploitation does not seem to have occurred to anybody engaged in it, though some were conscientious about the means. It was a truly Jupiterian age, paralleled in Britain only by the age of Elizabeth I. Queen Victoria succeeded to the throne in 1837, her

Sun/Moon conjunction in close sextile to the UK Jupiter, her Jupiter in Aquarius exactly conjunct the UK chart's ruling Venus, beautiful aspects in any synastry. One could say that nation and ruler mutually stimulated each other's capacity to expand, explore and pursue new possibilities. On Victoria's own chart Jupiter and Uranus are in mutual reception and form a wide (6½ degree) sextile. The scene was set and the explorers emerged, among them Sir Richard Burton.

Burton was as unlikely a figure as his chart suggests, a ruthless, swashbuckling megalomaniac, with a love of shocking and a passion for pornography, and yet a romantic. He was also a brilliant but completely undisciplined scholar. The multiple conjunctions present great complexity: one could describe the T-square in many different ways, depending on which planet one chose to start with. He was born against the background of the Uranus/Neptune/Pluto/Jupiter square, his Sun slotting right into it, so that he particularly embodied

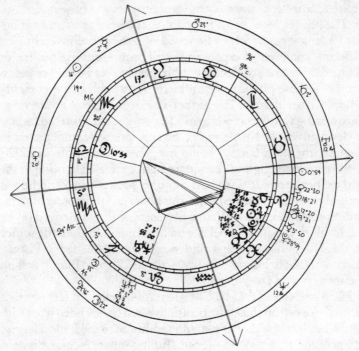

*Chart 2*
Sir Richard Burton: 19 March 1821, 9.30pm LMT, Hertford (51N48, 0W04). Progressions for 10 September 1853 — Arrival at Mecca.

the strangely explosive quality of his generation: rebellion through disintegration and destructiveness likely to come to expression through the urge to expand and explore, free from constraints. Burton's Sun in Pisces is elusive, hard to pin down, always ready to adopt an identity — Pisces is a favourite sign among actors, and Burton was particularly fond of disguises. Jupiter, I feel, adds to this liking for dressing up, and Sun conjunct Jupiter in the fifth tends to be flamboyant, the more so with Jupiter in self-declaring Aries, and as the Sun rules the MC the pose was a very public one. He combined a love of show and swagger with the Scorpio and Sun/Pluto penchant for secrecy and subterfuge. He had the strength and stamina of Scorpio rising and a battling Plutonian spirit, not unmixed with paranoia, which made him numerous enemies, whom he attacked bitterly. With Sun/Jupiter square Uranus he hated having to stay long in one place: any constraint imposed by the 10 degree Jupiter/Saturn conjunction was vigorously fought or wriggled out of. The Jupiter/Mercury conjunction manifested as an astonishing gift for languages, of which he was said to speak twenty-eight plus dialects — one way of expanding one's communicative powers, or of broadening one's outlook through speech — as well as a ceaseless flood of verbose publications and letters; he published over eighty volumes in his lifetime. The Jupiter/Pluto conjunction ensures that the questing spirit proceeds in hidden ways or encounters darkness or destructiveness. Numerous of his missions were undertaken in disguise, the most famous being his penetration of Mecca in the guise of a Syrian pilgrim, the square from Uranus delighting in the outrage perpetrated. With Sun conjunct Jupiter and Pluto he was brazenly concerned with exercising his power and promoting himself, and nowhere more bitter than when successfully challenged (as he was by his rival explorer Speke, who beat him in finding the source of the Nile), but perhaps underneath it all he had a Piscean uncertainty about his own identity — the real Richard Burton behind the mystery and fancy dress.

His wife claimed that he had such strong religious feelings that he used to weep on those rare occasions when he attended mass with her. Whether these are her romantic additions to the Burton legend or a genuine expression of the Sun/Jupiter square Neptune is hard to say. Certainly the Neptune square also led to degeneration through alcoholism. His could never have been a simple faith free from conflict, with Jupiter's aspects to Pluto, Uranus and Saturn; the Moon, ruler of the ninth, is also of course enmeshed in the T-square. He was a rebel and non-conformist in religion as he was in other respects. What curious mixture of religious passions could have been involved in his decision to make his perverse pilgrimage to Mecca? He claims to have shouted rude words in defiance of Allah at his shrine, like a blasphemous child, but he was hardly doing this out of outraged Christian convictions, as he steered largely clear of the Church until his deathbed, when his wife triumphed by having him convert to Catholicism — though some rumoured maliciously that he was already dead at the time.

The transits and progressions are for the approximate time of his arrival in Mecca. Pluto has progressed to the *exact* conjunction with the Sun, most appropriately for this secret mission which was to bring him fame (the Sun rules the MC). Mercury was active by progression for much of his life, going retrograde over Jupiter, Sun and Pluto before returning, and was now again conjunct Jupiter; his mastery of Arabic for this expedition was a great feat. Neptune and Uranus transits and a lunar progression pick out his Venus/Mars conjunction: his capacity to beguile his companions played a more important role now than at any time. And both Pluto and Saturn form aspects to the Neptune/Uranus conjunction, and also to the UK Jupiter. His outrageous deception not only brought him fame but flattered the national ego at this time of colonial expansion.

While Burton may have shown some degree of Libran charm, his wife seems to have mainly lived out his Moon in Libra in the eleventh on his account, oiling the social wheels for him, inhibited (opposition to Saturn) yet gushing (opposition to Jupiter). The Venus/Mars conjunction in Pisces is romantic, idealistic and very seductive. With Saturn opposition Moon and semi-sextile Venus he kept his women under control.

Lady Isabel Burton was no doubt expected also to embody his Taurus on the cusp of his seventh, a counterweight to his adventures. He seldom allowed her to travel with him — she must stay, representing the settled way of life for him as long as he was able to travel, providing him with the backup he needed, the organization and funding for his trips, and a home of some sort where he could write up his travel journals for publication. She must be tied so that he could be free. Perhaps she even represented that which he wanted to be free *from*.

The person who feels compelled to keep on the move often has

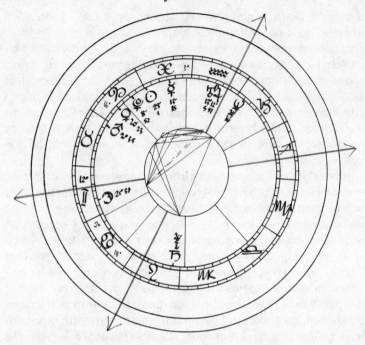

*Chart 3*
Lady Isabel Burton: 20 March 1831, 8.50am LMT,
London (51N32, 0W07).

no rosy picture of home life such as is offered by a contented and
emotionally supported childhood. Burton's Moon/Saturn suggests
such a lack, and Aquarius on his IC reflects the many sudden moves
that characterized his early life and deprived him of a sense of
belonging. Thoughtfully, his wife had his last resting place built
in the form of the most provisional kind of lodging: a desert tent.

Had Isabel Arundell been born a man, she declared, she would
have *been* Richard Burton, but being a woman she could find no
better fate than to be Richard Burton's wife. The exact Jupiter/Uranus
in her tenth house declares this aspiration to identify publicly with
the figure of the unrestrained traveller. It forms a semi-square to
her Sun, a trine to her ascendant and a wide trine to her Moon: at
every level of her being that freedom-seeking, masculine urge was
to be met. As Jupiter rules the seventh it was natural for her to seek
these qualities in a partner, and she had been waiting for such a

figure to enter her life since adolescence, but she did her utmost to live them out herself too, eager to share her husband's travels when he allowed it, but when this possibility was closed she adapted uncomplaining to merely basking in his glory.

Intensely romantic (Sun Pisces sextile Neptune, Moon quincunx Neptune), she had been told by a gypsy that it was her destiny to marry a man called Burton, and to spend her life in wandering, change and adventure with him. They were 'one soul in two bodies'. The conjunction of their Suns, only two minutes apart, reflects this feeling of identification. Mercury, the ruling planet of this naturally communicative lady (ascendant and Moon in Gemini) falls on Burton's Venus/Mars conjunction, and indeed she made it her responsibility in her own and their joint publications to give voice to Burton's own romantic side, which tended to be obscured by his coarse behaviour and sexual obsessions. Despite all evidence to the contrary she insisted on his gentle, even sensitive side, claiming for him such virtues as kindness to animals, which was certainly something she valued more highly than he.

Her Venus in Aries describes an approach to relationships more forward than was considered ladylike, and her unkinder critics have suggested that the marriage proposal came more from her side than from his, but Venus's location in the twelfth house suggests her self-less devotion to her partner, and one may also read into it the clandestine nature of their marriage. This eventually took place, contrary to her parents' wishes, when progressed Venus had reached the square of Saturn, signifying a binding of the affections and bringing into manifestation the loyal commitment inherent in the natal trine between the two planets.

Neptune in the ninth, picked out at the time of the wedding by minor transits from Jupiter and Uranus, suggests a romantic image of travel as well as a mystical/devotional attitude towards religion, and in her case an interest in spiritualism and matters psychic, and its sextile to the Sun and square to Mars heightens her yearning for a more than ordinary destiny and a more than ordinary man. Transiting Neptune is closing in to conjunct her Sun at the fulfilment of this dream. The progressed ascendant/descendant squares Pluto, indicating that she has to find an entirely new relationship between self and partner, constituting a period of drastic readjustment in her life, a rebirth — no doubt accompanied by the most intense feelings — into a new role.

The fourth house Saturn suggests that one of her motives in eloping with this wild adventurer and opting for a life of excitement and movement was reaction against parental authority and restrictive home life. Could it be that her tenth house Jupiter/Uranus conjunction picks up an unlived urge for excitement on the part of her mother, in counterpart to the constraining influence of a Saturnian father? At the time of the wedding, Isabel's ruling Mercury has progressed to the square of that unruly conjunction, which was no doubt stimulated in Burton's company by the trine from his Moon. It is also at this time further stimulated by a transiting sextile from Mars. The marriage, ruled by Jupiter, was certainly rather unconventional.

Burton is better described by the Sagittarius on her descendant than she by his Taurus descendant, which part she played with some reluctance, but she willingly accepted the fate of the rover's wife with its long separations, until advancing years confined them together to work on the written records of his travels. Ever eager to promote Burton as she would have had him (her own wide Sun/Pluto conjunction no doubt playing a part) she burned all his manuscripts after his death, preserving as best she could for posterity the image she clung to.

The ninth house link between travel and religion is not chance. It is difficult to talk about the spiritual life of the individual without using travelling metaphors: the *path,* the *Way* or Tao, a spiritual *trip.* Christians try to *follow in the footsteps of Christ;* Buddhist scriptures talk of *crossing to the other bank,* and Buddhist teachings are referred to as *vehicles.* A pilgrimage is an enactment of an inner process, with all its uncertainties and dangers. Even Burton's curious pilgrimage reflects spiritual concern, albeit of a perverse order.

In the life of Burton's contemporary David Livingstone the themes of travel and religion were inseparable. His birth time is unfortunately not known, but his extremely close grand trine of Sun, Jupiter and Uranus is eloquent. Having gone to Africa as a missionary, Livingstone found he could neither be satisfied working at an established post nor follow the trail of others, such as that of his missionary father-in-law Moffat, saying that he 'had not come to Africa to be suspended on the tail of anyone'.[4] A deeply religious man, it was important to him to convince himself that in going his own independent way (Sun/Uranus) he was fulfilling the intention of God, and he saw himself as a pathfinder and prospector for future missions. Interestingly, his Sun is in the same degree as Burton's and similarly,

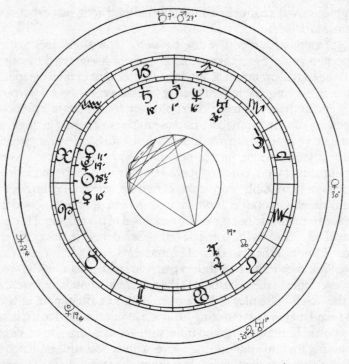

*Chart 4*
David Livingstone: 19 March 1813 (solar chart — noon GMT),
Blantyre near Glasgow.
Transits for 3 November 1871 — Meeting with Stanley.

though much more widely, conjunct Pluto. He showed the Piscean
quality of concern for suffering and the ability to identify with others
in a more sensitive way than Burton, but he also had the slipperiness
of that sign, being able to attract prospective sponsors for his missions
by appealing to their cupidity rather than their conscience and
dissimulating to the London Missionary Society his intention of
leaving the organization until he had other sources of finance lined
up. The Sun conjunct Pluto and square Mars gave him the strength
and courage required for his exploratory enterprises, and he made
as bad an enemy as Burton, being beset by a similar Plutonian
paranoia that destroyed many of his working relationships. Though
largely gentle with people, he was ferociously irascible and was capable
of beating unruly subordinates with any handy instrument. His

aggression was channelled into cultural and religious expansion (Sun/Mars/Jupiter).

Apparently his mood swung between depression (does Saturn aspect an angle? He was certainly known for his reserved manner) and the eternal optimism of Sun trine Jupiter. One of his biographers refers to his 'unquenchable capacity for discovering a good purpose in every hindrance he met';[5] he could even see the loss of a precious medicine chest in the malaria-ridden jungle as a blessing in disguise. But here we begin to run into Jupiter's problematic side. Livingstone's faith in God became increasingly faith in himself as the chosen instrument of God, enjoying special protection, and he did indeed have some remarkably good strokes of fortune, narrowly evading death many times. On one occasion, for example, he apparently owed his escape from hostile Boers to the breakdown of his waggon. He once remarked: 'We seem immortal till our work is done.'[6] In this confident remark one may hear an echo of Firmicus Maternus' lofty claim that men would be immortal 'if the favorable influence of Jupiter were not overcome in their charts'.[7] At the time of his most famous rescue at the hands of Stanley (3 November 1871, just after noon, at Ujiji on Lake Tanganyika) transiting Jupiter had just returned to his natal position in Livingstone's grand trine, with Venus in sextile from Virgo, opposing his Sun and forming a kite. This is beautiful evidence of Jupiter's protective influence. But the explorer was inclined to read into such incidents confirmation of his own unfailing rightness and came to feel himself scarcely capable of error, and to be correspondingly intolerant of the errors of others. Those of his colleagues who crossed him or did not share his vision became God's adversaries. Thus does the sense of a divine mission hubristically elevate a man in his own estimation and permit him special liberties. With a strong Jupiter it can be hard to be humble. Livingstone's journeys were no doubt journeys of the soul as well as of the body, but the spiritual quest carries with it the danger of spiritual pride, and it does not seem that he altogether avoided this.

Livingstone's Jupiter is within three degrees of the UK Jupiter, and had progressed to within one degree of it by the time his exploits captured the imagination and bolstered the pride of the British public. Jupiter and Uranus were conjunct the UK Jupiter when the news arrived of Livingstone's delivery at Ujiji.

The name of Livingstone is frequently twinned with that of Henry M. Stanley, who went in search of the long-missing explorer, probably

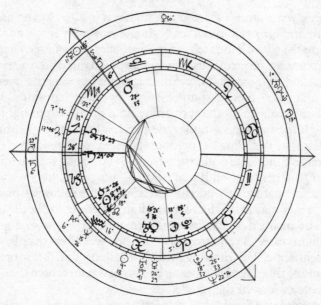

*Chart 5*
Henry M. Stanley: 28 January 1841, 5.45am (speculative) LMT,
Denbigh (53N11, 3W25).
Progressions for 3 November 1871 (noon LMT Ujiji) — Meeting with
Livingstone.

saved his life, and brought back news of him to an eagerly waiting
public. His birth time is given as between 5 and 6 a.m., and I have
taken a speculative time of 5.45, as the angles at this time fit in with
several major life developments.

Henry M. Stanley (né John Rowland) was an odd character who
fought his way to prominence from a background of massive
disadvantage. Born illegitimate in North Wales in the third year of
Victoria's reign, his father was killed (reputedly in a pub brawl)
around the time of his birth and his mother abandoned him. His
first years were spent with his grandfather, a butcher, who died when
the child was 5, and after nine months of living with a neighbouring
couple Stanley was consigned to the workhouse, an establishment
every bit as harsh as those described by Dickens.

Those with Saturn rising tend to feel that they have been born
into a rather unfriendly world which they need to protect themselves
from, and are generally inhibited and particularly shy in youth.

Stanley's Venus, ruler of the fourth house, is squared by the rising
Saturn, indicating a bleak early home environment, and her
conjunction with Uranus tells of inconsistency and sudden change
in that context. Jupiter in his own sign and his natural house, sextile
the Sun and trine the Moon, and the Sagittarian ascendant, however,
go a long way towards compensating for these hardships, and
furthermore offer a means of escaping from them. Saturn right on
the angle in Sagittarius would try desperately hard to be, or appear,
confident, while foiling the naturally positive, easy-going style that
Sagittarius rising would otherwise enjoy. To the strong twelfth house
Jupiter (planets right on house cusps — using Placidus — always
seem to me particularly potent in relation to the following house,
though they may make themselves felt in the preceding house too)
I am also inclined to attribute his extraordinary talent — a great
asset in his career as a journalist — for being in the right place at
the right time. His meeting with Livingstone was the supreme
example of this. Like Livingstone he also had rather more than his
fair share of luck in the jungle.

The sextile to Saturn and the ascendant from Mars — widely
conjunct the MC, which it rules — accentuates the need to work
hard to overcome obstacles and be seen to be a man. It also contributes
to Stanley's violent streak, along with the wide Mars/Pluto opposition
and Moon/Pluto conjunction. This conjunction also speaks of the
strong survival instinct he needed in the jungle.

The Sun in Aquarius indicates a man with a mind of his own,
and its conjunction with Neptune symbolizes the missing, idealized
father he was fleetingly to glimpse in the man who adopted him
as an 18-year-old immigrant in New Orleans, giving him the name
of Henry Morton Stanley and dying shortly afterwards, and later
in Livingstone himself. I notice that Livingstone's Chiron is exactly
conjunct Stanley's Neptune, and while I am unsure of the relevance
of Chiron in this context I do know that strong contacts to Neptune
from another person's chart tend to create a kind of yearning for
that other which cannot wholly be fulfilled. Stanley's happy months
in Livingstone's company were brief, and once again he lost that
illusive father-figure. His grandfather had died when the progressed
Sun came to within one degree of Neptune.

During the period in which Stanley worked his passage to America,
turning his back on the land of his birth, which he was subsequently
extremely reluctant to acknowledge, and was adopted into another

short-lived family, transiting Pluto hovered on his IC. Ten years later, now a successful journalist, he was sent by Gordon Bennett, editor of the New York Herald, to find the vanished Livingstone in Africa, going via Egypt, Turkey, Persia and India to pick up a few other stories. In this kind of enterprise Stanley was in his element, with his Jupiter square Uranus and Saturn rising in Sagittarius, aspected by Mars. He had been fairly constantly on the move since leaving the workhouse, and had travelled through plenty of testing situations. By this time Jupiter had progressed to within half a degree of the exact square to Uranus (and trine to Pluto). At the hour he received his commission the Moon formed a trine to his natal Jupiter.

Once again the strong Jupiter/Sagittarius element manifested in Stanley as faith as well as the desire to explore. But the simple faith that he had acquired with his bible in the workhouse took some heavy knocks when he encountered the brutality and injustice of the world (Saturn rising in Sagittarius, Jupiter trine Pluto, Mars in the ninth).

Stanley's progressed Jupiter was closing in on the aspects to Jupiter and Pluto and was in semi-square to Mercury, ruler of the seventh, when he met Livingstone in Ujiji. The Jupiter/Uranus conjunction of that time was in his seventh house, and coming into opposition with its ruler, Mercury. The only other transit involving Jupiter is that planet's quincunx to the rising Saturn in Sagittarius, so that with the progressed Moon at the end of Taurus it briefly forms a finger of god, pointing to the prime source of his outstanding achievement. Progressed Mars is now closely conjunct the Scorpio MC, with the progressed ascendant in square and transiting Saturn in sextile. It was the fulfilment of his fame as a tough adventurer, but he was soon to be embroiled in a public battle with London's Geographical Society which spoiled his triumph. The same planets of course also aspect the IC: the sore issue of the father who never stayed around was there again.

About the life of our last traveller I know almost nothing, but his chart is included in relation to his most famous journey. Thor Heyerdahl was the leader of the Kon-Tiki and Ra expeditions, both reconstructions of early voyages in vessels of types in use long before the keeled ship. The transits and progressions are for the time of departure of the Kon-Tiki expedition, which sailed from the Pacific coast of South America to Polynesia. Again, the exact birthtime is unclear, an alternative time of 4.40 p.m. also being proposed. This

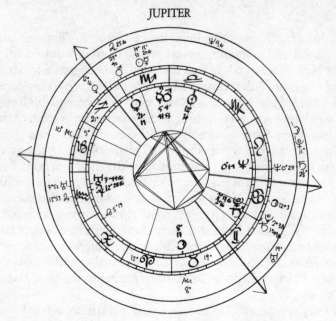

*Chart 6*
Thor Heyerdahl: 6 October 1914, 3.45pm (time disputed), Larvik
(59N05, 10E02).
Progressions for 28 April 1947 — Kon Tiki expedition.

would give Aquarius rising and put the Jupiter/Uranus conjunction
in the twelfth house. In either event, Jupiter rules the Sagittarian
midheaven, and is conjunct Uranus in Aquarius, close to the position
of the same conjunction on Isabel Burton's chart. Again, as in the
case of Stanley, the aspect between the two planets is backed up by
a certain emphasis on the signs they rule. Of the two, Uranus alone
is fully integrated into the tough fixed grand cross, but both planets
are in trine to the gentler Libra Sun, Jupiter exactly so. As the
expedition set off, his progressed Moon formed a grand trine with
Sun and Jupiter, easing him on his way, and progressed Venus was
on the Sun/Jupiter midpoint, in exact sextile to both. Progressed
Mercury forms slightly wider aspects to them, and squares progressed
Jupiter. The Sun is further invigorated by a progressed semi-square
from Mars, and progressed Sun is just moving out of square with
progressed Jupiter. The natal trine is also picked up by transits from
Pluto and Mars, while in the version of the chart printed, Jupiter
is transiting the ninth house, and progressed Mars conjuncts a ninth-

house Venus. If there was a time in Heyerdahl's life which an astrologer might have recommended for an important journey, surely this was it.

## Notes

1. J. E. Cirlot: *A Dictionary of Symbols,* trans. Jack Sage, Routledge & Kegan Paul, 1971 (1962).
2. Lao Tzu: *Tao Te Ching,* 2, XLVII, trans. D. C. Lau, Penguin, 1963, p. 47.
3. Constantine Cavafy: *Ithaka,* translated from the Greek by the present author.
4. Oliver Ransford: David Livingstone: *The Dark Interior,* John Murray, London, 1978, p. 26.
5. Ibid. p. 111.
6. Ibid. p. 109.
7. Firmicus Maternus: *Mathesis, Liber Secundus,* XIII, 6, trans. Jean Rhys Bram, Noyes Press, Park Ridge, New Jersey, p. 43.

## DATA

| | |
|---|---|
| Bob Dylan | Lois Rodden: *American Book of Charts.* |
| Charles Baudelaire | *American Book of Charts.* |
| Constantine Cavafy | Bibliographic note by G. P. Savvides in *Poems (1896-1918),* Ikaros, Athens, 1963, which gives 17/29 April 1863, Alexandria. |
| Isabelle Eberhardt | Astrological Association Data Section: 17 February 1877, 6 p.m. LMT, Geneva. |
| Thomas Cook | *Encyclopaedia Britannica:* 22 November 1808, Melbourne, Derbyshire. |
| Moon Landing | *Encyclopaedia Brittanica:* 20 July 1969, 8.17 p.m. GMT. |
| Orville Wright | *Encyclopaedia Britannica:* 19 August 1871, Dayton, Ohio. |
| Wilbur Wright | *Encyclopaedia Britannica:* 16 April 1867, near Millville, Indiana. |
| Kitty Hawk | Charles Harvey in *Mundane Astrology,* Aquarian, 1984: 17 December 1903, 10.35 a.m. EST, 36N02, 75W42. |
| A. de Ste-Exupery | Astrological Association Data Section: 29 June 1900, Lyon, France, 9.00 a.m. Paris Time. |

| | |
|---|---|
| Queen Victoria | Lois Rodden: *Profiles of Women:* 24 May 1819, 4.15 a.m. LMT, London. |
| United Kingdom | Charles Carter: *An Introduction to Mundane Astrology,* Fowler, London, 1951: 1 January 1801, 0.00, Westminster. |
| Sir Richard Burton | *American Book of Charts.* |
| Lady Isabel Burton | Lady Isabel Burton & W. H. Wilkins: *The Romance of Isabel Lady Burton: The Story of Her Life,* Hutchinson, London, 1897, p. 14. |
| David Livingstone | *Encyclopaedia Brittanica.* |
| Henry M. Stanley | Jadwiga M. Harrison: Fowler's Compendium of Nativities, Fowler, London, 1980, confirmed by the publishers as unamended. |
| Thor Heyerdahl | *American Book of Charts,* DD Section. |
| Isabelle Eberhardt | Astrological Association Data Section. |

**PRINCIPAL SOURCES CONSULTED**

Michael Hastings: *Sir Richard Burton: A Biography*, Hodder & Stoughton, 1978.

Oliver Ransford: *David Livingstone: The Dark Interior,* John Murray, London, 1978.

H. M. Stanley: *Autobiography*, Sampson Low, Marston, London, 1909.

Ian Anstruther: *I Presume: H. M. Stanley's Triumph and Disaster,* Geoffrey Bles, London, 1956.

Lesley Blanch: *The Wilder Shores of Love,* John Murray, London, 1954. (Sections on Lady Isabel Burton and Isabelle Eberhardt.)

# 7.
# Faith

Once upon a time there was a devout old Tibetan woman. She had a son who was a merchant and who, from time to time, undertook the perilous journey to India. Each time he set off she would beg him to bring her back a relic of the Buddha to strengthen her faith. The son, though well-meaning, again and again forgot his mother's wish as his mind was preoccupied with business and with the dangers of the journey. At last the old woman grew desperate, and threatened to kill herself if her son should return again without the desired object. As he drew near to home after his next journey he realized that he had once again neglected his mother's wish. Seeing a dead dog at the side of the road, he removed one of its teeth and wrapped it in a cloth, and this he gave to his mother on his return declaring that it was a tooth of the Buddha. The old woman gratefully took hold of the tooth and immediately gained enlightenment.

Tibetan story

'Seek and ye shall find', says the gospel, promising that the earnest quest shall not be in vain. Faith keeps us on the road, but what when we have *found* and are overwhelmed by a sense of deep conviction, this is right, this is it, I need look no further? This too is the province of Jupiter. To have faith is to be persuaded, and we can follow this line of thought at least as far back as ancient Greek *peithesthai,* to believe, from *peithein,* to persuade. The experience of faith in something specific is one of having been persuaded or convinced, there being no longer any room for doubt. By keeping faith we understand an attitude of unswerving loyalty. Being faithful means not running after other men/women/gods.

Yet here is a paradox. If any planet has to do with faith it is Jupiter, 'the natural Significator of Religion' according to Lilly,[1] but faithful . . .? We all know the type so full of enthusiastic promises forgotten next day. The conviction of the moment is such a powerful force that past experiences of waning enthusiasm and loss of interest are far from consciousness at such times.

Faith too is sometimes a fickle friend. Many volumes have been written on the subject, innumerable methods developed for encouraging and maintaining faith, yet it remains a gift of grace, not to be coerced into showing its face by any act of will-power, emerging unbidden when and where it pleases, sometimes even from the depths of suffering and despair.

I have mentioned already Jupiter's title of 'the guru' in Hindu astrology.[2] The guru is one who gives spiritual teaching, whom we trust to guide us, and it is often said that the true guru is within, but first we usually have to meet that figure in the outside world and project our own potential spirituality onto it. It is also said that when the pupil is ready the teacher appears. Whether this means that the teacher is always there if we but open our eyes to see or that he or she is attracted into our vicinity by our state of readiness remains a mystery, but at a certain point the inner state meets the outer figure, and the sense of rightness of that moment of meeting has been described by innumerable followers of the spiritual path.

Ma Prem Tao, whose chart is shown on page 69, with Moon and ascendant in Sagittarius and Sun sextile Jupiter, is both a woman with considerable resources of optimism and an untiring seeker. In the early 1970s she was an enthusiastic participant in that most Jupiterian of phenomena, the 'Growth Movement', which promised through the techniques of humanistic psychology endless expansion of consciousness and change for the better. Throwing herself wholeheartedly into one type of growth work after another she eventually came, like many others, to seek something of a more ego-transcending nature, and at that point she encountered the guru.

Jupiter in Tao's chart lies in the seventh house, and being the ruling planet it lends this house a special emphasis. Moreover he is in square aspect to Venus in the ninth. Thus the carrier of faith and promise is in the house of the Other, the house of partnership, and the planet

of attraction and relationship is in the house of the Path, and the
two are bound together as an image of the spiritual friend or beloved.
The Great Benefic seldom graces the seventh house in the manner
we like to expect with the partner showering us permanently with
all good things. Tao's marriage was not of long duration — duration
is not one of Jupiter's strong points — and once freed from this tie
she poured her fiery energy into a succession of meaningful but fairly

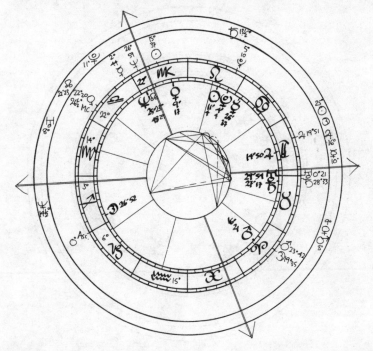

*Chart 7*
Ma Prem Tao: 3 August 1941, 4.00pm, Toronto (43N42, 79W25).
Progressions for 16 June 1977.

brief relationships, always drawn again into pursuing that elusive
divine quality in another person and seldom indulging long in regrets
over separating paths.
     At the time of her third Jupiter return a cluster of progressed and
transiting aspects heralded the constellation of the spiritual friend.
The Sun had now progressed from the sextile to the square of the
seventh house Jupiter, and transiting Neptune opposed him, to bring

an element of spiritual yearning into the picture. The ninth house
Venus, the friend in the realm of spirit, was receiving a transit from
Uranus, signifying a sudden development in relationships, and the
transiting north node was also conjunct progressed Venus exactly.
Transiting Pluto in sextile to her Sun announced the end of a chapter
in her life, a clearing away for new developments. On 16 June 1977
the transiting Sun squared her Neptune; Venus and Mars, conjunct

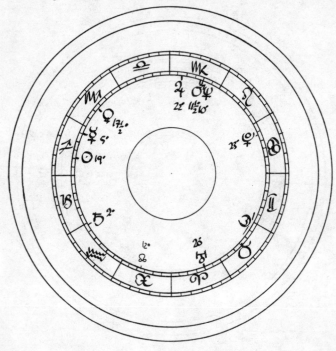

*Chart 8*
Bhagwan Shree Rajneesh: Solar chart: 11 December 1932, Jabapur, India.

in the house of love affairs, trined her Venus, and Sun, Moon and
Mercury were in her seventh house. On this day, shortly after arriving
at his ashram in India, she formally became a disciple of Bhagwan
Shree Rajneesh. Though she had little personal contact with him,
he was in a sense the ultimate partner, whom she spoke of with love
and commitment. The Moon's nodes on Bhagwan's chart form a T-
square with the Sun, Mercury, Mars and Neptune, and this picks
up Tao's own Jupiter/Venus square. Bhagwan's Jupiter conjuncts the

fateful point of Tao's north node, and also her Neptune, where it stimulates her longing to lose herself in the divine. With his Mercury in Sagittarius (conjunct her ascendant) he was an inspired speaker, and poured out stories gathered from a wide range of spiritual paths to feed her Jupiter in Gemini. Jupiter of course is in his detriment in this rather sceptical sign, and this position, when emphasized, produces a lot of inner struggle and questioning over matters of belief. Tao herself stresses that her teacher encourages doubt and is grateful to him for pushing her to question. She feels strongly the danger of falling into blind faith and prefers the word 'trust' to describe her feelings towards him.

Some readers will have doubts about the qualifications of the particular guru in question, but this is not the issue here. People can believe in things which to others are phoney and be immeasurably enriched, and they can believe in things others generally agree to be admirable and behave abominably, witness the Inquisition. Faith is not a guarantee of some sort of objective truth, it is not necessarily reconcilable with reason, it is not necessarily moral, but it is a powerful force in itself. In Tao's case there can be no doubt about the authenticity and transforming quality of her experience; and to this the chart is testimony.

Before leaving Tao's chart I would like to point out one thing more. Saturn by transit, just removing his leaden weight from her Sun, is about to enter the ninth house. I have repeatedly found Saturn's transit through the ninth to correspond to commitment to a spiritual path of some kind, and this is hardly surprising. Here he pushes us to fix the volatile substance of our spirituality, to hold fast to our faith, contain it in some kind of structure, build it into our lives. Unfortunately it is scarcely possible permanently to anchor our faith in this way, but on the other hand commitment and discipline are necessary for any kind of spiritual development.

The sign of Sagittarius belongs to the traveller, the seeker (who by definition never arrives), but also traditionally to the Church itself, to those deemed to have found, and respected for proximity to God, Jupiter's colour being the bishop's purple. It is usually to a figure recognized as carrying the power of a spiritual tradition that we turn for guidance in such matters. Paul Huson[3] connects Jupiter with the Tarot card known as the Hierophant, the 'revealer of holy things', spiritual father and priest, and tradition advises us that Jupiter inclines towards religious professions. But the Jupiterian qualities of tolerance and openness to new things are difficult to maintain when one is committed to, or even a representative of, a given teaching. Jupiter is at once the youth who would be free of ties and Father Zeus whose word is law, he is both unreliable and tyrannical, playboy and authoritarian, seeker and proclaimer of doctrine, and even in the announcement of the latest enthusiasm the Jupiterian individual can come across as extremely dogmatic.

The role of the religious teacher is a difficult one, for such an individual must carry the projections of those who see him or her as the embodiment of spirituality, and this is a considerable load. The congregation do not gather together in the name of the Lord to hear the priest express his doubts. They go to be uplifted and renew their faith, and his task is to encourage and assist them in this, to plant in their minds something positive, preferably inspiring, to sustain them through the week. To this end he must speak with conviction. But like other human beings the preacher must have his moments or periods of doubt, and how does he face his flock at such a time? Probably he will banish all dark thoughts and speak with a little more emphasis as he strives to convince his listeners and himself. Here lie the roots of the Jupiterian failing of hypocrisy, which means play-acting — the object of which is to suspend disbelief. 'Thus the priest often has no alternative but to be the hypocrite now and again, to hide his own doubts and to mask a momentary inner emptiness with high-flown words. If his character is weak, this can become a habitual stance.'[4]

The individual who has a vocation to assist others in their faith has no monopoly on hypocrisy, despite being in the front line in the war against doubt. I imagine that all of us at one time or another have experienced the person who must at all costs convince us that he or she has the Answer, whether it be the missionary with a foot in the door, or the converted friend. The thought that may formulate itself in the recipient of such an onslaught of enthusiasm is something like 'The lady doth protest too much, methinks' or 'Who are you trying to convince?' The truth of the matter is that we are nowhere more vociferous in challenging the unbelievers around us than when we are unwilling to give quarter to our doubts. A salesman may make an excellent job of promoting products, apparently believing wholeheartedly in them at that moment, and next week peddle rival wares. He has to be convincing because his livelihood depends on it, while the peddler of beliefs has a somewhat less conspicuous gain from convincing others — it is further proof of the validity of those beliefs. According to a research report of the Church of Light[5] 92 out of 100 charts of salesmen had a prominent Jupiter, the planet also associated with religious professions. My experience suggests that the most dogmatic individuals are usually those who have Jupiter not only prominent but heavily afflicted, and frequently in mutable signs, from which one might deduce considerable inner conflict and instability in matters of faith. This is, of course, not to say that a Jupiter with hard aspects is necessarily dogmatic, but that dogmatism is one of the ways of counteracting such insecurities.

We have run again into the slippery side of Jupiter, ruler of Pisces which, while associated with the twelfth house and the devotion of the religious recluse, is also the sign of deception. It is not only Neptune who leads us into the pleasant illusions of wishful thinking but Jupiter the gullible, his face turned towards the light, no need to look over his shoulder. Charles Carter, very astute on the less attractive side of Jupiter, which is greatly to his credit since he had a strong Jupiter himself, has the following to say:[6]

> A. J. Pearce, writing in Victorian times and himself a native of Sagittarius, copies out most of Lilly's laudatory adjectives, but entirely omits any reference to an 'unfortunate' Jupiter, apparently wishing to persuade himself and others that such a condition does not exist!
>
> Here Mr Pearce exhibits clearly one of the weaknesses of Jupiter, to wit a dislike of facing up to and acknowledging unpleasant facts, especially about one's self! Most of us have met the sort of person who will believe anything provided it is agreeable, and that is the stamp of an uncontrolled Jupiter.

People's gullibility in the area of religion has probably been exploited since time immemorial, and a favourite method is by offering the Jupiterian carrot of later rewards. In this the cult supporters squeezing out their last ounce of energy to raise funds for their Leader, whom they expect soon to create heaven on earth, resemble the Templars and the present-day young warriors of Iran, hurling themselves into battle and almost certain death to gain entry into Paradise. I do not mean to suggest that there is no Paradise, only that in the realm of Jupiter there are no proofs and we open ourselves to deception from within and without if we do not tread here with caution, alert to the possibilities of bluff, empty rhetoric and seduction.

' "Legitimate" faith,' says Jung,[7] 'must always rest on experience,' and this means that faith simply based on external authority is likely to let us down. The rituals designed to help us develop faith can gradually become habitual and lose their meaning. Blind faith can lead one into all sorts of unholy actions, but even this is easier than facing the lonely inner struggle. One individual who wrestled with his own doubts was Martin Luther, who also challenged the authority

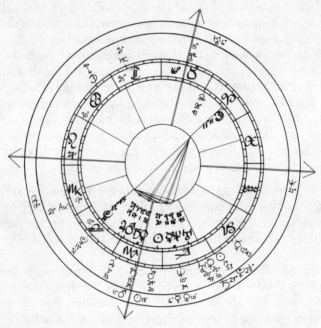

*Chart 9*
Martin Luther: 10 November 1483 (Old Style), 11.00pm LMT, Eisleben (51N32, 11E32).
Progressions for 31 October 1517.

of the religious tradition he had been brought up in, and particularly attacked the exploitation of people's gullibility through such practices as the granting of indulgences.

Luther's chart has the Sun and three other planets in Scorpio and the Moon in Mars's other sign, suggesting someone who does not avoid confrontation. His Leo ascendant exactly squares the fourth house Sun, with Jupiter in the third in exact sextile to the ascendant and semi-sextile to the Sun. While the semi-sextile is perhaps not in itself a very strong aspect, when it is as exact as on Luther's chart any transit will aspect both planets together, and in this case the ascendant too. According to one school of thought the planet which most closely aspects the Sun indicates the likely profession of the native, and in this case it is Jupiter; the Sun has no major aspects to any planet. When Luther decided to enter the religious life, at the time of his first Uranus square, transiting Neptune was in 27 degrees of Capricorn, aspecting Jupiter, Sun and ascendant. Neptune transits often open us up to spiritual dimensions, but there were other things going on too. Apart from the Uranus square, the progressed Sun was conjunct Uranus and the transiting Sun on the day of his resolve (2 July 1505)[5] in quincunx to Uranus. It was indeed a sudden decision. Caught in a thunderstorm and in a state of terror he promised St Anne that if she protected him he would become a monk, and this he did within days. As is generally the case with Uranus transits one cannot really put this promise down to the impulse of the moment. The thought had probably been fermenting away inside him for some time, but it was fear of death that pushed him into this commitment, and with the weight of fixity on his chart he was not one to wriggle out of it. He said later: 'not freely or desirously did I become a monk, but walled around with terror and agony and sudden death, I vowed a constrained and necessary vow'.

By progression his Jupiter had now completed the exact conjunction to Mars in Scorpio, and religion was experienced in life or death terms. Progressed Mars was on the IC: obviously a change of residence was on the cards, and I wonder if he was also inspired by anger towards, or feelings of competition with, his father (note the loaded fourth house) to break with his past and presumably take on a spiritual father. At all events, it was on his way back from a visit to his parents that he took his vow.

I remarked above on the tendency of Saturn transits through the ninth to correspond to commitment to a spiritual path. It should not be forgotten that transits in the ninth follow on from transits in the eighth, where they often coincide with emotional crises, broken relationships and experiences of the dark side of life. Never is the need to find meaning in life so urgent as when one touches despair, and close proximity to death can often be the catalyst that enables us to make that breakthrough. That Uranus had just entered Luther's eighth house at the time of his encounter with death is also significant.

Luther's decision may look somehow accidental, but he was clearly a deeply religious person. Nevertheless he suffered from severe guilt and doubts, which can probably be attributed to Scorpio's attunement to the more savage levels of human nature, and also to Jupiter's conjunction with his Mars. Mars disposes of both Sun and Moon, and is himself in Scorpio, so Jupiter and all he symbolizes, such as faith, hope, spiritual freedom, is caught up in the need to do battle, and in the third house we might have guessed that this would ultimately mean a battle of words.

A turning point came in Luther's life when, desperately seeking an answer to his doubts he came upon the words in the New Testament 'the just man shall live by faith'. At this his problem dissolved and he had a feeling of being born again. Unfortunately it is not known when exactly this moment of faith came to him, but the date on which he pinned his ninety-five theses on the door of All Saints' Church, Wittenburg, is well-known; it was 31 October — All Saints' Eve, or Hallowe'en, 1517. No doubt the Church planned All Saints' Day to coincide with and absorb an earlier pagan festival, but there has always seemed to me something piquant about that juxtaposition of the night of shades and witches and the day of all that is heavenly and holy, and it seems to me that the choice of this dramatic moment reflects something fundamental in Luther's character expressed by the Sun in Scorpio on the one hand and the Leo ascendant and Jupiter in Libra on the other. Certainly there is a dramatic note in this configuration, and a struggle between the shadowy and the bright. We connect Scorpio with areas taboo in our culture, those things not accepted into the light of day, and in thirty years of nearly continuous transits through that sign we have dredged a good many of them to the surface, but to Luther in the sixteenth century, a celibate man of god, with a Leonine sense of nobility and Jupiterian aspirations, the realm of seething human passions must have seemed the abode of the devil.

On this Hallowe'en in 1517 (the chart is progressed to this date) Saturn was in 27 degrees of Sagittarius, aspecting Sun, Jupiter and ascendant. Saturn transits are testing times, times, as we have seen, for commitment, for facing up to what has to be done, and at this point Luther was standing publicly by his faith and representing the faith of the individual against the authority of the Church. His progressed Sun and transiting Pluto were sextile Mars (conjunct Jupiter in the third, remember) and he declared war. I suspect that the complex flavours of the planets in the fourth house (the father) have something to do with his attitude towards authority, and also the Saturn/Venus conjunction, which, although in the third, conjuncts the IC. Saturn had now progressed to the IC, perhaps building up for several years a concern with the paternal authority of the Pope and Luther's spiritual roots in tradition. His progressed Mercury in sextile to Venus no doubt helped him to find the right words. He must have been a powerful speaker with the punchy and persuasive conjunction of Mars and Jupiter in the third, and the inspirational conjunction of Mercury and Neptune in Sagittarius, rendered more urgent by the sextile from Pluto on the third cusp. He was also a prolific writer, and a polemical one.

The remainder of Luther's life was a struggle against the Catholic church, which excommunicated him three years after his defiant act, and on 18 April 1521 he is reputed to have affirmed defiantly before the Diet of Worms (the words may be apocryphal) 'Here I stand, I can do no other.' His Mars had now progressed to 27 degrees of Scorpio, conjunct the Sun, semi-sextile Jupiter and square the ascendant. There must be an element of doubt about the exact angles of the chart, but if the time is not correct these transits and progressions stress all the more the importance of the Sun/Jupiter semi-sextile. There is something aspecting these points at each step in his career as a man of God. Neptune was at 27 Sagittarius when he became a monk, Uranus at 27 Pisces when he was ordained a priest and conducted his first mass in May 1507, the progressed Sun at 27 Sagittarius when he obtained his doctorate in theology (October 1512), Saturn at 27 Sagittarius at the posting of the ninety-five theses that marked the beginning of the Reformation, and progressed Mars at 27 Scorpio at his public trial.

For the Sun/Jupiter individual faith is an important ingredient in life, as is the desire to go beyond what is experienced as confining — restrictive laws, current limits of understanding, the prison of the flesh or of worldly concerns. Faith itself in fact produces a sense of liberation from such bonds, for with God all things are possible. It is characteristic of Jupiter to wish to share such freedom and shower it on others. Jupiter's generosity, and for that matter his wastefulness, come from a sense of abundance which spills over, and Luther's eagerness to spread his insights is backed up by Jupiter's conjunction with the militant Mars in Scorpio. Where Mars is involved in a man's chart his very masculinity is at stake, and as Luther was at this point

still celibate (he married later) one can imagine that his considerable
sexual energy was channelled into his mission. The military monastic
orders such as the Templars, the Teutonic Knights and the order of
St John who flooded the twelfth and thirteenth centuries with blood
were doing something similar on the level of brute force, but Luther
came along at the time when Northern Europe was ready for a new
kind of spiritual campaign.

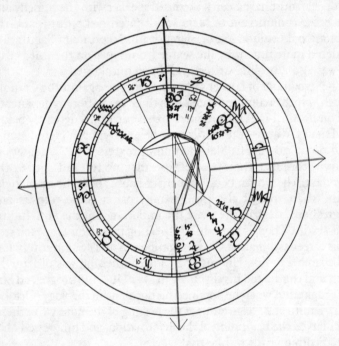

*Chart 10*
Billy Graham: 7 November 1918, 3.30pm EST, Charlotte, NC
(35N13, 80W51).

The combination of spiritual aspiration and fighting spirit is not
unusual, at least in Christianity. Arguably the origins of the 'Onward,
Christian soldiers' attitude do not lie in Christianity itself, but in
the Church's need to harness the brutality of a military artistocracy
still rooted in the war-enthusing cult of Woden, with Valhalla rather
than Heaven the hoped-for resting place of the warrior. At all events
this combination is still potent, and the war against sin is still a popular
evangelistic theme.

The chart of Billy Graham, veteran campaigner for Christ, is again dominated by Mars and his signs. General William Booth has the Sun and two other planets in Aries, the Sun being in trine to Jupiter in Sagittarius. In the chart of another nineteenth-century evangelist known as Billy Sunday, the close conjunction of Mars and Jupiter appears again, in Scorpio and conjuncting the ascendant from the twelfth house, with Sun and Mercury also in Scorpio. This chart positively shouts about the Good Fight, but as there is uncertainty about the correct time I will not indulge in further analysis, though feeling that the chart looks highly appropriate.

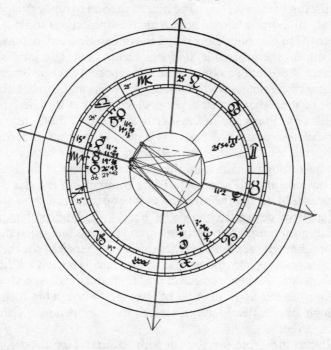

*Chart 11*
Billy Sunday: 19 November 1863, 6.00am LMT (time disputed), Amers, Iowa (42N02, 93W37).

Billy Graham has Sun, Mercury and Venus in Scorpio, Aries rising and Mars, the ruler, in Sagittarius in the ninth, conjunct the Moon and MC — another fighter's chart. The Sun is closely trined by Jupiter in the fourth, which in turn carries the waning effects of a conjunction with Pluto. The emphasis on Scorpio in these three charts, combined with the sense of hope and promise afforded by Jupiter, reflects a deep concern with redemption from sin and doubt through the experience of spiritual rebirth. Though Graham's work predates the current vogue for the expression 'born again', this is one of the essential themes of his work, and as we have seen Luther had such an experience himself. Graham's Sun is not only in Scorpio but also in the eighth, urging him towards fulfilment through confrontation with darkness. The origin of sin is seen as the Fall, and the cause of the Fall, says Graham quoting the gospel of St John, was 'the lust of the flesh and the lust of the eyes . . .'.[9] The trine of the Sun to Jupiter suggests a strong supporting faith to sustain such confrontations and inspire others. 'Man is a contradiction. On the one side hatred, depravity, and sin; on the other side kindness, compassion, and love,' says Graham,[10] no doubt aware of these two opposing forces in himself.

Jupiter is in the fourth in Cancer — the caring spiritual father. I have no idea what Graham's personal relationship with his father was like, but Pluto also in the fourth and close to the IC hints at dark experiences in that area, or of a need to blot out something unacceptable in Graham's early experience or family background, perhaps through a shift from the destructive father to the Father in Heaven. Jupiter/Pluto contacts are common on the charts of religious leaders, but the meaning of the two planets is poles apart — Zeus never descended into Hades' realm — and the combination implies great tension between the two and the possible achievement of faith through the encounter with death and despair — the theme of transits moving from the eighth into the ninth again. It is a difficult combination, this juxtaposition of the bright and the dark, and even a dangerous one as the example of Jim Jones, who led his disciples through faith to death, shows. He had the conjunction in Cancer in the seventh.

Mercury in Scorpio, in a T-square with Saturn and Uranus, suggests a forceful, urgent style of communication, if not a particularly easy flow, but Mercury is widely trine the ascendant too, and this is helpful in putting things into words. The semi-sextile from Moon and Mars in Sagittarius adds vehemence.

Words are the instrument through which the missionary conveys the good news and attempts to bring the heathen from darkness into light, but the word 'crusade', which originally meant destroying the infidel with the sword, is still appropriate in this context. It is the attempt to abolish the collective shadow and no doubt, as these charts imply, the personal shadow too.

Where there is brightness there is always a shadow, and one of the features of Jupiter that we experience as benefic is his ability through his sheer brightness to blind us to that reality, to induce in us a state of blind faith in which all evil, all possibility of being mistaken is banished — and usually projected onto those who believe differently. This is a condition to be found in many a religious organization or spiritual community where 'negativity' in members is frowned upon and they are encouraged to protect themselves from contamination by avoiding contact with those who might be critical. The community is described in such images as that of a 'city of light' in a dark world. This sort of identification is flattering to the ego, for who does not wish to be one of the elect, one of the few who have got it right? The borderline between positive thinking and inflation is hard to define, and it is just in this territory that Jupiter's persuasive salesmanship can lead us astray.

And one last thought on the subject from Nicholas Culpeper: religion can damage your health: 'If [the cause of the distemper] be Jupiter, it comes through religion, some idle Priest hath scar'd the poor creature out of his wits.'[11]

## Notes

1. William Lilly: *Christian Astrology,* Regulus, 1985, p. 612 (original edn 1647).
2. See note on p. 33.
3. Paul Huson: *The Devil's Picture Book,* Abacus, 1972, p. 154ff.
4. Adolph Guggenbuehl-Craig: *Power in the Helping Professions,* Analytical Psychology Club of New York, 1971, p. 23.
5. Doris Chase Doane: *Astrology: Thirty Years of Research,* Professional Astrologers Incorporated, Hollywood, 1956.
6. Charles Carter: 'Jupiter the Planet of Progress', *Astrology,* quarterly of the Astrological Lodge of the Theosophical Society, vol. 18 No. 2, London, 1944.
7. C. G. Jung: *Symbols of Transformation,* Collected Works Vol. V, Routledge & Kegan Paul, 1956, para. 345.
8. Data on Luther's life are taken from the *Encyclopaedia Britannica,* 1974 edn.
9. Billy Graham: *How to be Born Again,* Hodder & Stoughton, 1977, p. 53.

10. Ibid. p. 51.
11. Nicholas Culpeper: *Semeiotica Uranica*, 1655 ed, London, p. 107.

## DATA

| | |
|---|---|
| Bhagwan Shree Rajneesh: | Date only, from a disciple. |
| Martin Luther: | Lois Rodden: *The American Book of Charts,* Astro Computing Services, San Diego, 1980. |
| Billy Sunday: | Ibid. Dirty Data Section. |
| General William Booth: | 10 April 1829, Nottingham, England. Ibid. Dirty Data. |
| Billy Graham: | Michel and Françoise Gauquelin: *The Gauquelin Book of American Charts,* Astro Computing Services, San Diego, 1982. |
| Jim Jones: | 13 May 1931, 10.00 p.m. CST, Lynn, Ind. *American Book of Charts.* |

# 8.
# Vision

When we say that someone has vision we mean that he or she can see something that others cannot. We are talking about a seeing with some inner faculty that is not bound by the senses. An entrepreneur who sees a potential market for a product not yet made may be said to have vision. Again it is the province of Jupiter, the ability to go beyond what is given, to leave the beaten track, a process which involves risk. Granted that for business a powerful sense of realism, a good support from the earth element is also needed, a strong Jupiter or Sagittarius influence is a great help in finding the way forward to bigger and better things. Transits and progressions to natal Jupiter tend to mark the point where such a vision opens up. Conrad Hilton, for example, invested in the hotel chain that was to become the basis of a business empire in a year which saw by transit the north node conjunct, Uranus and Saturn square and Jupiter trine natal Jupiter.

To have *a* vision, however, generally implies something much less materialistic, and something far less open to proof than the capacity for free enterprise. Those who see visions are in the grip of something more powerful than the ego, something numinous, but how can we evaluate it? Sagittarius may be involved — the visionary poet William Blake had Sun conjunct Jupiter in Sagittarius — yet this is Piscean territory too, and Neptune is usually also involved. Here nothing can be measured, and nothing can be brought back from that other world to satisfy the sceptic.

Religious establishments tend to vet claims to divine visions with care. How can one know where they come from: from God? from the Devil? from a sick mind, or an over-strong imagination? from some change in body chemistry? From the point of view of a church, such visitations are valid only if they can be interpreted in the light of established doctrine, and then only if the seer of the vision demonstrates a proper attitude of humility and obedience. But in this mysterious domain, who can truly judge? The visions which are recorded for us are generally those which catch the popular imagination, which through the meaning they have for the seer send wider ripples into the community.

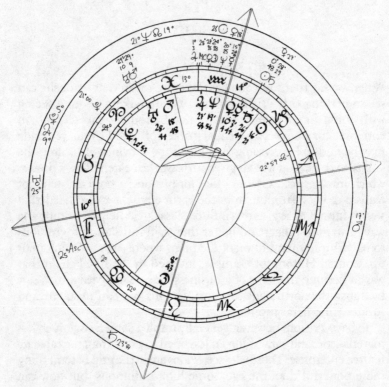

*Chart 12*
Bernadette of Lourdes: 7 January 1844 LMT, Lourdes (43N07, 0W03). Progressions for 11 February 1858 — First vision.

The chart of Saint Bernadette of Lourdes demonstrates both the importance of Jupiter in such cases, and also the Jupiter/Neptune connection. Here the two planets are conjunct (albeit widely) in the tenth house. It is the visionary combination *par excellence*. Carter[1] mentions someone with this conjunction who 'saw fairies'. Whether we believe in God or in fairies is beside the point. There is ample evidence that individuals with Jupiter/Neptune contacts are susceptible to experiences which appear to come from 'other worlds', but it is doubtful whether through astrology we can explain or judge such experiences.

With her Sun in Capricorn, just over 10 degrees from Saturn, we can assume Bernadette to have been an essentially serious girl. Indeed, she is described as having had a simple, matter-of-fact approach, and this came out during the interrogations she underwent about her visions. She showed the firmness and clarity of the two Saturnian signs (Aquarius is strongly emphasized and contains her ruling Mercury), never exaggerating and always insisting upon plain accuracy, remaining clear-headed in the face of attempts to confuse and misquote her. She was articulate (Gemini rising) and weighed her words carefully (Mercury conjunct Saturn). Capricornian too was the way in which she was to endure without complaint chronic ill health, pain and hardship. The Geminian ascendant comes over most strongly in her liking for playing tricks on people, and her disarming sense of humour, as well as in a tendency to talkativeness (Moon opposition Mercury, too), which she had to learn to curb when she eventually took up her vocation as a nun. The difficult and explosive combination of planets in the eleventh house was reflected in the problems she experienced in fitting into a communal convent; there were occasional outbursts, and she acquired a reputation for touchiness and more especially of stubbornness (Aquarius again, and Leo Moon).

The moment that changed her life came at the age of fourteen. She was out collecting wood with two friends on 11 February 1858 when she had a vision of a lady in white. There followed a sequence of visions, and the apparition eventually identified herself as 'Immaculate Conception'. The transits and progressions on the chart are for the day of the original vision. There must remain an element of doubt as to the accuracy of the birth time, but the exact conjunction of the progressed midheaven with natal Jupiter is startling, and it seems likely that progressed angles would be involved in such a major turning point. But even if we ignore the progressed midheaven, progressed Venus is also conjunct the Jupiter degree. Discarding for a moment the religious explanation, we might see in this coming together an opening up or revelation of Bernadette's own feminine side, but clearly the experience was of something more than the personal, a revelation of a cool, purified, Aquarian feminine, a gentle yet remote vision of the most highly treasured feminine image of her culture. The progressed Moon, that other most feminine planet, is a few degrees away, on the Jupiter/Neptune midpoint, while the transiting Sun falls between the natal Neptune and progressed Moon. Jupiter by transit closely squares the natal Moon, echoing the theme.

The location of so much of this activity in the tenth house ensured that it became a public affair. With Jupiter (and Neptune) in the tenth natally, her faith and her vision were necessarily to be manifested in that aspect of herself which was turned towards the world. When the midheaven progressed to meet Jupiter (as I am inclined to believe) the adolescent became publicly stamped as a visionary, and at the same time her reputation suddenly grew out of all proportion to her youth and humble origins. The tenth house passage of the progressed Moon in itself reflects concern with being in the public eye. Despite the joy of the visions themselves, the immediate notoriety she acquired at this time and her subsequent fame with its attendant danger of inflation were a force to be reckoned with throughout her life. Her progressed Mercury had also turned retrograde within the year, conjunct the midheaven. She became a spokeswoman, a messenger. What she conveyed was a message to the Catholic public and the Catholic Church that the doctrine of the immaculate conception of Mary had the seal of divine approval, for those long words meant nothing to the poor and illiterate 14-year-old — she had to keep repeating them to remember them — but they meant a great deal to the clergy; the purity of the Virgin's own conception had been declared dogma three years earlier. Saturn in Capricorn in the ninth on her natal chart is a further indication of the importance in her life of the established church, which was to embrace her visions and canonize her.

Her Capricorn Sun had progressed into Aquarius to form a semi-sextile to progressed Jupiter as she was initiated into a new sense of the divine purpose in her life. It was also, incidentally, in exact quincunx to natal Chiron in the fourth, and this must surely correspond to considerable disturbance to her home life. Transiting Neptune had just left the semi-sextile to its natal position, implying a time when she was particularly open to intangible influences, and its semi-sextile on the other side to eleventh house Pluto tells of the disruption her visions created in her life as a member of a small community; her childhood friendships must have been drastically changed.

Saint Teresa of Avila, whose chart has a Jupiter/Neptune trine, with the Sun in sextile to both, took up the religious life as a young woman, but was just one nun among many until the age of 40, when she had a powerful experience of conversion while looking at a picture of the Passion. This appears to have opened up her inner eye, and thereafter she saw many visions. The numerous transits and

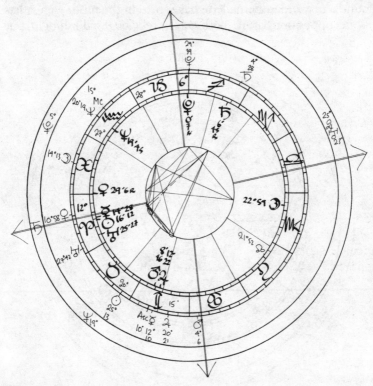

*Chart 13*
Teresa of Avila: 7 April 1515(NS), 5.30am LMT, Avila (40N39, 4W42).
Progressions for 1 July 1555 — Year of conversion experience.

progressions to her chart around this time, which I do not intend to discuss in detail, bear witness to a major life turning point. Of particular interest in the context of this book is the completion by progression of the Jupiter/Neptune trine and the fact that progressed Mercury, having reached the almost exact conjunction with natal Jupiter, went stationary retrograde that year. It is also possible that

the ascendant joined in that conjunction. Mercury natally is conjunct
the ascendant and sextile Jupiter in Gemini. As with Bernadette,
Teresa was in some sense a messenger, and this was the year when
she appeared to open up that divine channel of communication.
A woman of action (Sun and ascendant in Aries) and now an ardent
believer (ruling Mars conjunct Jupiter), her new insights led her to
found a new order. Bernadette has Saturn in the ninth, Teresa has
Jupiter opposition Saturn; both suggest religious establishment, but

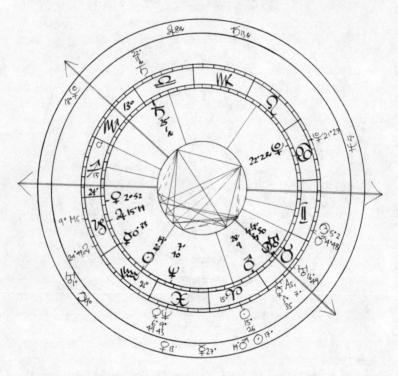

*Chart 14*
Emmanuel Swedenborg: 8 February 1688(NS), 5.30pm LMT, Stockholm
(59N20, 18E03).
Progressions for 7 April 1744, 0.00hrs. — Vision.

Teresa was an Arien pioneer, with Uranus rising, too, and she
performed something of a revolution. The vision she was to fulfil
was that of a more simple and rigorous type of convent than those

that existed, where discipline was slack and luxuries were enjoyed. No doubt the Saturn opposition to Jupiter and ruling Mars played a part here, and the conjunction of those two planets falls in the second house. Poverty was to be a strict rule in the new order. Perhaps she was in part driven by the awareness and condemnation (Saturn) of her own potential for extravagance. Perhaps she felt that the fire of faith was sufficient security.

With Emanuel Swedenborg we move on to a figure who would have been doubly a heretic in the eyes of the Catholic Church. Son of a Protestant bishop of humble origins, his visions led him to establish a new church. There are conflicting accounts of his birth time, and he could have been born half an hour later with the ascendant in Capricorn, but I am inclined to accept the chart printed.

The Sagittarius ascendant with Jupiter in the first house goes with a keen traveller and seeker, but he did not find his true religious identity until his Sun came to square Jupiter. At that point the vision embodied in the Jupiter came to mean something deeply personal to him. He was a remarkable polymath, and a scientist (Sun Aquarius, earthy emphasis), but in science, in the natural physical world, he saw the spiritual everywhere. This is the great potential benefit of Jupiter in his fall, pragmatic Capricorn: spirit infusing matter. For Swedenborg the body was the kingdom of the soul, and according to his Doctrine of Correspondences, which was to influence a generation of symbolist poets, everything outward and visible in nature had an inward spiritual cause. There was no such thing for him as mere matter.

The transits and progressions are for the night of his first vision, which took place in Holland. Christ appeared before him and issued a rather obscure command, which led him to give up his current work and present a new revelation to the world. The new teaching which was to emerge was truly Aquarian in its humanism, abolishing original sin, vicarious atonement and eternal punishment, it offered man new freedom and responsibility. To Swedenborg's credit he at first questioned his experience and tested the vision, which required the presence of mind of his Sun Aquarius and the healthy caution of Jupiter in Capricorn, widely squared by Saturn. But it may also have come as a relief to be able to accept the voice of authority (Capricorn again).

The progressed Sun not only squares Jupiter but also sextiles the Moon/Uranus conjunction on the IC, which forms a close trine to

natal Jupiter and squares the natal Sun. Again this reflects the
revolutionary quality both of his nature and of his visions, which
perhaps also replaced the authority of his own father, who had himself
been Uranian in his attitude towards the establishment. Neptune
is brought into focus by the progressed conjunction of Venus,

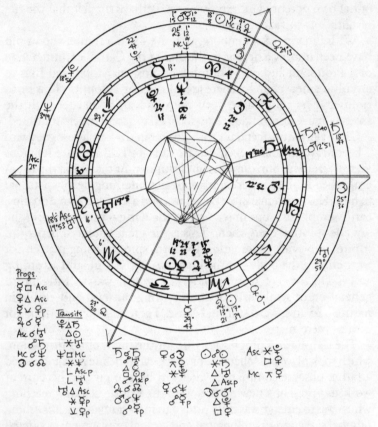

*Chart 15*
Aleister Crowley: 12 October 1875; 10.50pm LMT (speculative), Leamington
Spa (52N15, 1W40).
Progressions for 8 April 1904, Noon Cairo — Dictation of Book of the Law.

suggesting perhaps beyond the opening up of visionary experiences
a divine union and a flood of compassion. The progressed ascendant
sextiles Neptune, and the progressed midheaven forms the same
aspect to the progressed planet. By transit, Pluto trining the Sun

signals an end to his old sense of identity. Once again Mercury is involved; Uranus transits conjunct as the revolutionary message begins to break through. Jupiter forms a quincunx to Neptune, and Neptune is approaching the opposition of Jupiter.

Here too Saturn is in the ninth house natally, contributing to a grand cross. The Aquarius and Uranus elements contribute to the breakaway from the established church, but the struggle for a new establishment, under new authority, begins.

Aleister Crowley's chart may be something of a surprise at first glance. Sun conjunct Venus in Libra and Moon in Pisces is hardly what one expects in a black magician. On closer scrutiny, however, the elements, are there. The gentle, passive Pisces Moon is flanked by close sextiles to Mars and Pluto, while the Sun receives aspects from the hard planets Mars, Saturn and Uranus, with a wide quincunx from Pluto. Pluto is quite strongly aspected, though not quite as strongly as I had expected, and is in the eleventh house. This he lived out through numerous secret societies, which were frequently ruptured by power struggles in which Crowley participated. Saturn is in the eighth, the house of occultism and of sexuality, which latter consistently played a part in his ritual magic. Indeed, it is easy to read an element of sexual obsession into these rites, frequently dictated to him from 'other planes', concordant with the fear and fascination with sexuality often shown by Saturn in that house. It is however on account of the Mercury/Jupiter conjunction in Scorpio that the chart has been included. One might translate Jupiter in Scorpio as seeking the light in hidden ways. If one allows Mercury full participation in the grand cross, it is the only personal outlet for all the power inherent in the Saturn/Uranus/Pluto T-square which characterized his generation. Now Jupiter/Mercury is on the one hand inclined to produce a lot of words, and on the other to give voice to vision, being frequently met in the charts of poets.

The time of the chart is uncertain, the version printed being one of several proposed, and in my view likely to be correct given the six progressed and transiting aspects at the crucial date involving the angles. I suspect a Leo rather than a Cancer ascendant, to go by photographs and descriptions of his lordly behaviour. Having been initiated into various magical practices, on 8 April 1904, at 12 noon in Cairo, Crowley kept an appointment ordained by spirit messages and began to write down at dictation the mysterious *Book of the Law,* which declared him the prophet of the new age dawning.

The words claimed the authority of the god Horus. The number of progressed and transiting aspects are truly astonishing, even down to minor transits, which slot into place like cherries on a fruit machine when the jackpot is won. These I have listed, and leave in the main for the interested reader to explore. What is of interest in the context of this book is that progressed Jupiter has closed the conjunction with Mercury; it is exact to one minute of a degree. So Mercury/Jupiter

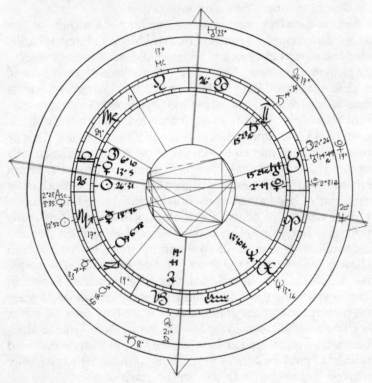

*Chart 16*
Arthur Rimbaud: 20 October 1854, 6 am LMT, Charleville (49N47, 4E45).
Progressions for 1 March 1871 — Approx. date of visionary experience.

manifests as the *book* of the *law*. It is the occult (Scorpio) word of the god, received in a voice inaudible to the world (opposition Neptune). I cannot claim to be a fan of Crowley's, but astrologically the event looks convincingly like the fulfilment of a strong and curious destiny.

The inspiration behind the brilliant and devastating poetry of the nineteenth-century French writer Arthur Rimbaud is expressed in his conviction that the true poet is necessarily a visionary, a *voyant*. His strongly aspected Jupiter is in the house of writing (the third) and in sextile to Mercury. This wayward youth, whose work profoundly influenced the generation of surrealist poets, had abandoned his writing career by the age of 21, probably indeed by 19.

The Sun, Moon, ascendant and ruling Venus all in Libra, idealistic, thirsting for aesthetic fulfilment, and for 'the Good, the True and the Beautiful', [2] were to clash dramatically with Pluto, opposing the Sun from the seventh house, experienced as violence, disgust, debauchery and self-destructiveness. His first encounter with the dark side of life came when he was 6, with the desertion of the family by his father, when his Sun had progressed to the exact opposition of Pluto and Uranus transited over his eighth house Saturn, ruler of the fourth. The chart speaks clearly of the experience of this loss as a death. A precocious scholar, the urge to explore implicit in his Sun square Jupiter was expressed not only in third house activities but also in early flights from home in search of adventure. In later life he was to become a traveller and trader in Africa.

At the age of 16½ on his third runaway trip from home, he had an experience that was to change him and his poetry drastically. What that experience was is a mystery, and it is often assumed that it involved an initiation into sexuality among the vagabonds of Paris, but certainly he returned home in early March 1871 shaken to the depths, raging, blaspheming and dirty, refusing to behave in a manner less than outrageous, and soon to express convictions of a poetic mission and produce poetry filled with powerful imagery and the struggle between good and evil. About two months after his return, he wrote two letters in which he expounded his theory of the poet as seer and the need to construct a new poetic language, based on laws as immutable as those of mathematics, in which the experience of all the senses could be expressed. The process of becoming a seer involved a 'long, immense and deliberate disordering of the senses'. Later he was certainly to use hashish in this pursuit, but it is not known whether his initial vision owed anything to drugs.

The chart is progressed to the approximate date of his illuminating and shattering experience. Since Jupiter is our focus, let us first look at Jupiter's natal aspects. Firstly he is in square to the Sun, signifying an urgent need to expand or explore in order to fulfil and express

himself; it marks him out as a seeker, as one who will not easily find
contentment. The square to the ascendant (the time appears to be
exact) is even closer: he has no choice but to live out the Jupiterian
role. The square to Venus suggests that relationships, aesthetics and
(as was evidenced in his later life) the desire for things material are
likely to be involved in this struggle for growth, this need to go beyond
the given limits. The sextile to Mercury echoes Jupiter's third house
position, and is a combination often correlated with the ability to
communicate vision through poetry. William Blake and Robert
Graves have the conjunction, Wordsworth the square. Here Mercury's
Scorpio position reflects Rimbaud's powerful and at times
unflinchingly savage use of word and image. Neptune in Pisces is
again involved by sextile, the planet of ego-loss, which Rimbaud
advocates, and of other realities, and Uranus is in trine. The
revolutionary call for a new poetic language (Mercury/Jupiter/Uranus)
struggles with Jupiter's placement in his fall in Capricorn, which
demands that his vision be made concrete, structured, planned
(compare Swedenborg), an intention which comes over in his famous
*lettres du voyant.*

With the progressed Sun in semi-sextile to Venus and progressed
descendant conjunct Pluto at this time, there was considerable focus
on relationships. An intense literary friendship Rimbaud had formed
with his teacher, Izambard, while progressed Venus opposed Pluto,
was about to break up, and his tempestuous relationship with the
poet Verlaine was soon to begin; then there is the likelihood of a
first (probably homo-) sexual experience. All other astrological
developments relate to his vision. Neptune is as heavily implicated
as Jupiter in the transits and progressions. The Sun has progressed
to trine Neptune, radical and progressed, while the progressed MC
forms the quincunx. It is an experience of disintegration, of
'disordering', and of yearning. Mercury has now progressed to form
a semi-square with Jupiter, pushing the glimpse of meaning into
verbal expression. The applying semi-sextile of Mars to Jupiter (54
minutes, but Mars tends to produce his effects early) tells of the violent
nature of the poet's insight, bursting through the normally cautious
style of Capricornian vision, while transiting Neptune squares Jupiter:
enough in itself, one might think, to suggest a visionary experience.
Uranus has just passed the opposition to natal Jupiter and now
opposes his progressed position, bringing in the element of revolution
and of sudden knowledge. Soon it would cross the midheaven, and

the poet would make his eccentric debut in Paris. The progressed Moon trines Jupiter from the house of dark secrets. Jupiter is just moving out of conjunction with Saturn, giving a sense of release from bondage. Progressed Mars is on the cusp of the third, and Pluto approaches the opposition of Mercury, as the poet's use of language is drastically changed. Saturn's transit through that house has for some time made writing a matter of serious concern to him. It is also undoubtedly of significance that Chiron is natally conjunct Jupiter, at 16° 25' of Capricorn.

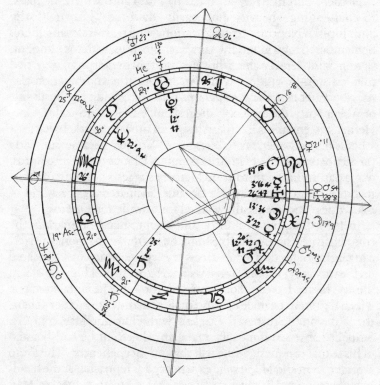

*Chart 17*
Hugh Hefner: 9 April 1926, 4.20pm CST, Chicago (41N52, 87W39). Progressions for 25 October 1953 — Approx. date of first publication of Playboy.

The potency of this revelation, that he was not only a poet but a visionary with a mission to create a new poetic language, inspired

Rimbaud for three years, perhaps a little more. Then he abandoned his literary pretentions and spent the rest of his life in travel, adventure and dealing. We shall never know whether he succeeded in finding a new vision.

From the heights and depths of poetry we return again to the world of business, to a man whose market vision grew out of his personal fantasy life. Hugh Hefner's enterprise became a multi-million dollar concern because he rightly estimated that his fantasies were shared by millions of men and dared to promote them.

Hefner's Sun in Aries, aspected by Pluto and, widely, by Mars, is challenging, heroic, not easily daunted; but it is the Sun/Jupiter/Neptune configuration which is relevant here. Remember that we found the same combination, with the same Sun sign in Saint Teresa's chart, but her fight, her enterprise, were tied to a less worldly vision. Mystical at its best, the combination also suggests Peter Pan, the *puer aeternus,* avoiding adult responsibility, or Walter Mitty, the dweller in dreamland, escapist, anti-realist. Only Hefner's ascendant is in an earth sign to provide a little ballast. At school he was seen as a dreamer. Writing became an early preoccupation: Mercury in Aries conjunct Uranus rushes into words, while Saturn in the third trine Mercury suggests a feeling of effort to prove himself verbally. He became fascinated by the world of magazines, and eventually worked for a while for *Esquire.*

In 1953, poor but optimistic and keen to make his mark in the competitive business of publishing, he borrowed the money to start a magazine of his own. The success of *Playboy,* which first appeared on the streets in October of that year, was to realize for him the dream lifestyle his readers could only enjoy vicariously. The fantasy was one which flattered the male ego and male sexuality. On Hefner's chart, the Sun is on the cusp of the eighth, with Pluto and Mars contacts. Sexuality obsessed him. Like many an adolescent he had boasted of his sexual conquests while still shy and inexperienced. The Pluto aspects to Sun and Moon were experienced as repression at the hands of his parents, and he saw himself as a champion taboo-breaker. Mars and Jupiter are in the fifth house, the house of fun. Of people with Mars in Aquarius Arroyo says, 'their attitude toward sex is often ultra-modern and experimental' [3]. With Jupiter, rather ostentatiously placed in this house, 'liberated' sexuality became not only his boast but, in his eyes, a philosophy if not a creed to be fought for. Uranus right on the descendant also figures in this need to be a revolutionary, to shock, and suggests why ordinary middle-class marriage (he had a try at this) did not satisfy him.

Yet in all this, as the strong Neptune and the Moon and Venus in Pisces convey, he was a romantic rather than a cynic. In the summer of 1962, as Uranus entered his twelfth house he retired to the inner world of his mansion paradise, where he remained for most of the 1960s, scarcely venturing outside. Here, protected from the rude world by a hierarchy of employees, he indulged his romanticism with an endless succession of pretty, girl-next-door sexual playmates, some of whom lasted for a number of years, most of whom were under twenty. He selected the centre spread 'playmate' for each issue of his magazine, and here his public and private life delightfully intertwined. It was a world like that in which the future Buddha's father tried to lull his son into forgetfulness, from which old age, death and poverty were excluded. In Hefner's pleasure palace no one was permitted to use the word 'no' to him: it was a browbeaten child's wish-fulfilling dream of permissiveness. The romantic in Hefner was blind to the exploitation of women involved, indeed he was wounded by such accusations. Both the Moon and Venus are in the most passive sign of the zodiac, and in the sixth, destined to serve. The bunnies, dressed to evoke the most soft and vulnerable of small animals and ever-obliging by order, fit the picture nicely. Perhaps the Saturn square to Venus indicates a need to keep women under control, for fear of allowing them too close.

The idea of *Playboy* magazine took shape during 1952, after Hefner quit his job with *Esquire*. During that year the Sun/Jupiter/Neptune configuration was touched in turn by transiting Neptune, Saturn and Jupiter and by progressed Mercury. The progressed Moon aspected the same planets slightly earlier, and Uranus took its turn in 1953. By October 1953, when the first edition of *Playboy* hit the streets, progressed Mars had crept up to stimulate Venus; one might expect a love affair with this development, and maybe in a sense it was. But Venus also rules the second (income) and the ninth (publishing). Hefner rapidly became a rich man. He had glimpsed the potential to exploit the collective fantasy and built on it. Saturn is again involved, in square to Jupiter and Neptune: he made his dream into an institution. But when the particular fantasy had become outmoded, his empire dwindled, and he was left an ageing man with an ageing dream.

Jupiter is a door opening onto something bigger, more fulfilling, more important, more profitable. Under transits and progressions to Jupiter that door opens sufficiently for us to glimpse what is beyond. This can often be the beginning of a major new development, and may have, as in the above cases, greater than personal significance.

## Notes

1. Charles E. O. Carter: *Astrological Aspects,* Fowler, 1972 edn, p. 147 (orig. pubd 1930).
2. From Liz Greene's apt descripton of Libra in *Star Signs for Lovers,* Arrow Books, 1980.
3. Stephen Arroyo: *Relationships and Life Cycles,* CRCS, 1979, p. 75.

## DATA

| | |
|---|---|
| Bernadette: | from Lois Rodden's *Profiles of Women.* |
| Saint Teresa: | *Profiles of Women.* Rodden in an *errata* sheet says that the chart should be recalculated for the Gregorian rather than Julian calendar, but the chart published is already Gregorian. |
| Swedenborg: | Lois Rodden: *The American Book of Charts,* Dirty Data Section. The times proposed do not vary greatly, and that used in this book seems to fit well. |
| Crowley: | *American Book of Charts.* Dirty Data section again. This time was apparently quoted in *Equinox.* Other times proposed range between 10.30 p.m. and midnight. |
| Rimbaud: | *American Book of Charts.* |
| Hefner: | Astrological Association Data Section. The chart had previously been published in the Gauquelin *Book of American Charts,* but erroneously calculated for CDT instead of CST. |

## PRINCIPAL SOURCES CONSULTED

René Laurentin: *Bernadette of Lourdes,* Darton, Longman & Todd, London, 1979.

André Ravier: *Bernadette*, Collins, 1979.
Signe Toksvig: *Emanuel Swedenborg*, Yale U.P., 1948.
Francis King: *The Magical World of Aleister Crowley*, Weidenfeld
& Nicolson, 1977.
Enid Starkie: *Arthur Rimbaud*, Faber & Faber, 1973.
Frank Brady: *Hugh Hefner, an Unauthorized Biography*, Weidenfeld
& Nicolson, 1975.

# 9.
# Politics

I have never heard Jupiter specifically associated with qualities of leadership, but he is named after the king of the gods, in horary he rules 'high places', and he is undoubtedly helpful in attaining positions of prominence. The reasons for this are not hard to fathom. The Jupiterian type, though sometimes obnoxious, is on the whole popular. Even in the relatively introverted, a strong Jupiter generally inclines towards sociability, indeed one modern astrologer[1] believes that Jupiter's function in natal astrology is primarily concerned with relating to others. While I cannot wholeheartedly embrace this account of the planet's role, I do not feel it is without foundation. Jupiter's energy pattern seems to be one that moves outwards, from a sense of inner abundance or confidence in self (or a good imitation of it) into the world around. One sees it in an openness to encounters and a willingness to reach out to others. A woman who came to see me amid a rush of Jupiter transits kept repeating: 'I feel I want to reach out to people'. Unlike the Saturnian type, who at parties shrinks into a corner or bears the proceedings stiffly, the children of Jupiter tend to spread a warm glow of geniality on such occasions, and are generally good at winning friends and influencing people.

I once heard Ingrid Lind remark that individuals with Sagittarius rising are good at interviews, and this I heartily endorse, adding only that a strong Jupiter also serves in such situations. There may of course be a good deal of bluff involved, but the person who comes across as confident has a head-start on rivals. A strong Jupiter also helps one to see the opportunities that present themselves, and to have the confidence to seize them. 'In politics you just seize your chances as they come, and make the most of them,' said Margaret Thatcher (Sun square Jupiter), 'and that's what I've always tried to do.'[2]

While other factors are required to contribute responsibility and powers of organization, Jupiter can lend a note of authority and conviction. It is particularly when the task in hand is a difficult one requiring a lot of Saturnian effort that a leader with vision is sought, one who can instil a sense of 'going somewhere', impart to team or party feelings of optimism, and rally enthusiastic support for the cause. In the last chapter I discussed the persuasive powers we expect in the preacher, but there are plenty of secular situations which require someone to point the way forward in a positive manner. I suspect that charts of successful military leaders tend to have Jupiter prominent — Napoleon, the Duke of Wellington and Montgomery of Alamein all have strong Sun/Jupiter contacts for a start — as the ability to inspire men under hard conditions is a vital component in such a figure, as well as the influence of Mars and his signs. The closing lines of Henry V's speech before the battle of Honfleur exemplify what is needed. Jupiter here mingles with Mars:

> For there is none of you so mean and base
> That hath not noble lustre in your eyes.
> I see you stand like greyhounds in the slips,
> Straining upon the start. The game's afoot:
> Follow your spirit; and upon this charge
> Cry 'God for Harry, England, and Saint George!' [3]

In the political sphere too the ability to command enthusiastic support is a vital factor, particularly in dismal times. In the run-up to the 1984 presidential election, Ronald Reagan declared himself to be the candidate of 'confidence and growth' (Sun square Jupiter) in contrast to his rival Walter Mondale, the candidate of 'fear and limits' (Sun Capricorn, exact semi-sextile to Saturn). In the face of such a choice, or even the appearance of such a choice, who is going to cast a vote for Saturn? There are times when caution and restraint would be wiser, but this is never a truly popular policy with the electorate.

Sun/Jupiter contacts are frequently found in the charts of political leaders. According to David Hamblin's reseach this shows up particularly in the fourth harmonic chart, and certainly the square aspect seems to be the most frequent. By and large the hard Sun/Jupiter contacts come across more strikingly in individuals than the trines. While someone with a Sun/Jupiter trine can take Jupiter's benefits for granted, the person with a square is as it were harassed by Jupiter all the time, cannot simply be him- or herself without the feeling creeping in that there is more to do, to achieve, to discover, to acquire. There is a compulsion to expand in some way, which may mean to become more important, and this can manifest as posturing and swagger, which quite often mask feelings of inadequacy. But it may also mean to open up new realms of thought — Sun square Jupiter is apparently also more common than average in the charts of philosophers.[4] Either way, Sun square Jupiter can be very productive, on the whole more so than the trine.

Like the preacher, the politician sometimes has to be convincing in times of doubt, promising election victories where none are expected and assuring the public that all is well when all hell is breaking loose behind the scenes. Perhaps it is the final recognition of the importance of this ability that, at a time when television exposes leading politicians to every voter, the citizens of the United States should have chosen in Ronald Reagan an actor to take on the leading role of President. Does Jupiter have a relationship with the acting profession? There certainly seem to be some connections: the ability to strike a pose and of course his rulership of Pisces, that most chameleon-like of signs. The Gauquelin research has found a tendency for Jupiter to cluster in the 'Gauquelin sectors' on charts of actors, peaking in the twelfth, ninth, sixth and third houses. My own research has found a distinct preference among actors for Jupiter in the twelfth or *fifth*. In the case of Reagan, the Scorpio-rising version of his chart gives Jupiter in the twelfth, the Cancer-rising version in the fifth. A 'hypocrite' — this failing is frequently attributed to Jupiter — originally meant an actor, and Michel Gauquelin also connects Jupiter with a liking for 'dressing up'.[5] This my observations agree with. Dressing up is a way of exploring different possibilities in oneself, and not necessarily superficially, and also of acquiring instant dignity, more impressive appearance, especially with uniform and robes. And the mythological figure himself had a liking for disguises. With Jupiter we can never be absolutely certain what lies behind the appearance, whether we are experiencing heartfelt sincerity, wishful thinking or a good performance, and his support is generally a boon to the politician for whom it is essential to present a convincing picture and win public confidence (even on his/her off-days). Those with poor presence in public tend to fall by the wayside, even though they may have considerable administrative ability.

There is some dispute about the correct chart for the United States of America, but I have no doubt that the correct version has Sagittarius rising, [6] and is therefore ruled by Jupiter. The sense of unlimited scope for expansion afforded by the vastness of the available territory is reflected in an economy based on continuing expansion and free enterprise and a population known not only for the all-American virtue of 'thinking big' but also for its physical stature: immigrants

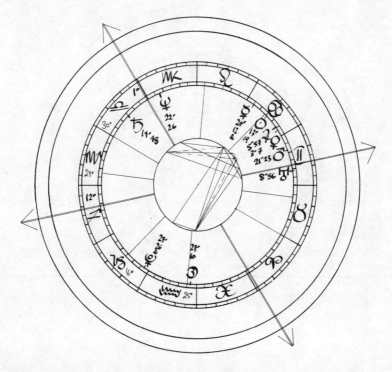

*Chart 18*
United States of America: 4 July 1776, 5.10pm, Philadelphia
(39N57, 75W08).

from countries where the population is normally of smaller build tend to produce children who are taller and better-built than themselves in the US. It is a society whose hero is the cowboy, the Sagittarian man on horseback, and in which the easy acceptance of limitations is frowned upon. In attaching the label of 'man of limits' to his opponent, Ronald Reagan was plugging into a current of

national revulsion. By its constitution, the United States is also a
country based on religious tolerance, although in practice Jupiter's
less flexible view of religion is not infrequently declaimed. Jupiter
on the US chart is in Cancer, in the seventh house, closely conjunct
Venus, and more widely the Sun. Venus/Jupiter is frequently self-
indulgent as Michael Baigent has pointed out in the context of the

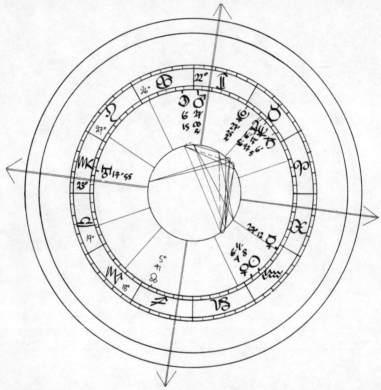

*Chart 19*
Franklin D. Roosevelt: 30 January 1882, 8.45pm LMT, Hyde Park, NY
(41N48, 73W54).

US map,[6] and a strong Jupiter can be wasteful of resources, and given
to conspicuous consumption. Wastefulness comes out of a feeling
of abundance, and I find it striking that during the depression the
people elected, as President, Franklin D. Roosevelt, who not only
has Sun square Jupiter himself but has three planets in exact aspect
(they are all within 20 minutes of exact) to the US Jupiter. Medically

and psychologically, the application of Jupiterian remedies and the cultivation of Jupiterian pursuits were traditionally recommended as an antidote to the baneful influence of Saturn. [7] It is precisely when things look black that we seek out a leader who will renew our optimism, and when we are forced to cut back we want a leader who will show us the way forward to new growth, and this might be expected to be particularly true of a Jupiter-ruled nation.

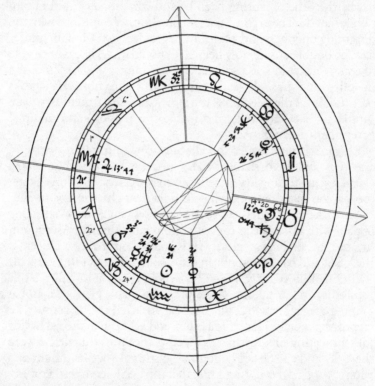

*Chart 20*
Ronald Reagan: 6 February 1911, 1.20am (time disputed), Tampico, Illinois (41N38, 89W47).

Ronald Reagan, a great admirer and one-time follower of F. D. Roosevelt, was also elected at a time of national doubt. The failed Vietnam War was not long in the past, followed by the economic instability caused by the oil crisis. After the scandal and shame of Richard Nixon's presidency, its term concluded by Gerald Ford, the nation not unnaturally turned to the alternative party and voted in Jimmy Carter. Carter had Jupiter in Sagittarius, conjunct the US ascendant and in wide sextile to his own Sun, but he failed to sustain public confidence. His failure to foil the Tehran hostage seizure ended his re-election chances. Reagan, who succeeded him, with a Sun/Moon/Jupiter T-square, and according to one version of his chart conjunct the ascendant, though of course bitterly opposed by many, has by the time of writing been by and large successful in raising public morale. The expansiveness of Sun/Jupiter combined with the disarming openness and expressiveness of feeling of Moon/Jupiter have no doubt considerably helped his popularity. He has been able to convey his vision of a still-expanding country and convince the majority that he will lead them in this direction. He speaks particularly for the freedom of the individual (Sun Aquarius, square Jupiter — like Roosevelt, who shared this passion) and minimal government interference.

Reagan's Jupiter trines the US Sun to within half a degree of exactness, and this describes well his success in boosting the national ego: if you are feeling low on self-esteem you can hardly find a better companion than someone whose Jupiter strongly aspects your Sun. 'They make each other feel good,' says Stephen Arroyo[8] speaking of pairs with interaspects to Jupiter from Sun, Moon or Ascendant, 'it's reciprocal.' Reagan clearly feels good about being a citizen of the USA, and has perhaps been inspired to seek great things by the tradition of his country. He is also a spokesman for morality, a role Jupiter is fond of taking — the preacher again. Here Reagan has found a great following, but has also attracted strong censure for identifying moral with political issues, and has been quoted as having told a meeting of Christian evangelists that the struggle between the USA and the Soviet Union was a 'struggle between right and wrong, good and evil',[8] and branded the USSR as an 'evil empire', an expression of utter political and religious conviction. Here again is Jupiter's frightening face: his eagerness to identify exclusively with what is right and moral, helped here, perhaps, by Scorpionic suspicion. Reagan's identification with the 'right side' is the stronger for those citizens old enough to remember his movie career: in fifty-three films he was only once a villain, another expression of his Jupiter trine to the US Sun. The US Sun is in Cancer, and Reagan's views hark back to the old-fashioned family values dear to traditional America. His style also touches the sentimental at times, which seems

to go down rather well. Reagan's Jupiter is in Scorpio, even if the
ascendant is not, lending a certain toughness and fighting quality
to his views and expansive tendencies. If the Cancer-rising chart is
correct, Reagan's ascendant is closely conjunct the US Jupiter, but
I have not found those angles to show up under progressions. The
version published here is the Scorpio-rising one.

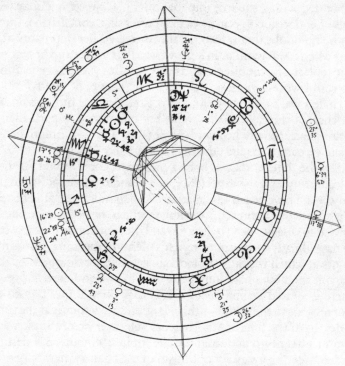

*Chart 21*
Margaret Thatcher: 13 October 1925, 9am GMT, Grantham,
(52N55, 0W59).
Progressions for 15 June 1982.

Margaret Thatcher became Prime Minister of the United Kingdom
at a time when Britain's economic power and influence were in sad
decline. Her Jupiter again square the Sun, and Mars, forming a T-
square with Pluto, showing her to be a woman capable of fighting
for her beliefs. The martial strain is reinforced by her Scorpio
ascendant. Although with Saturn rising in that sign her style was

severe, she nevertheless conveyed to many of the electorate an air
of confidence and vision. 'I feel there are times when we have lost
our vision of the future, and we know that where there is no vision
the people must surely perish,' she had said a few years earlier. [9] Like
Reagan she also took a strong moral stance. Her moment of glory
came in 1982 when Argentina siezed the Falkland Islands and she
responded with a show of imperial might. However one may feel
about her decision to pursue victory rather than conciliation, there
can be no doubt that it considerably increased her popularity at a
time when it was waning. In her own words: 'Doubts and hesitation
were replaced by confidence and pride that our younger generation
too could write a glorious chapter in the history of liberty.' [10]

There were a number of interesting transits and progressions to
her chart at the time of this event, but one transit in particular is
relevant here. Natally, her North Node (1°28′ Leo) in the ninth house
of foreign parts is conjunct the UK Jupiter, which being in Leo (2°52′)
and in the tenth indicates both a preference for a Jupiterian style
of leadership and the expectation of a grandiose role for Britain in
the world. I have no pat explanation of the significance of the nodes.
The humanistic approach according to which the north node points
forward to what we need to develop and the south node back to what
we have already made our own yields plenty of meaning, but as the
points at which the Sun or Moon are eclipsed, or devoured by the
dragon, the nodes have long been held in awe and even in dread.
There is a fated feeling about events that occur under transits or
progressions to the nodes — there is often such a transit at the time
of death. At the time of Mrs Thatcher's election victory, Jupiter was
conjunct her north node and the UK Jupiter: a moment of destiny
for her meeting a wave of optimism in the country, new hopes for
the future. At the time of the victory of the British task force in the
Falklands, Uranus trined this point and Jupiter squared it. Britain's
shrinking economic significance made it the more important for many
Britons to see their tenth house Jupiter impressing itself on the
international scene. The fact that Argentina had not only invaded
but was also ruled by a military dictatorship meant that the British
feeling of being in the right went hand in hand with a view of the
UK as the champion of liberty, always a favourite picture held by
the British of themselves: Uranus was not only involved by transit
but is in exact sextile to Jupiter in the UK chart and conjunct the
ascendant.

I am certainly not the first person to remark that Jupiter is strongly placed in the charts of leading Nazis, sometimes predominantly well-aspected as in the cases of Hitler and Himmler, and people are prone to mention this with some puzzlement. I suspect that this is because though many of us pay lip-service to a mode of interpretation which describes chart features in terms of *ease* and *difficulty*, we have not shaken off an earlier viewpoint which judged such things as *good* or *evil*, words which though they were not necessarily always understood in moral terms are nevertheless those primarily used to

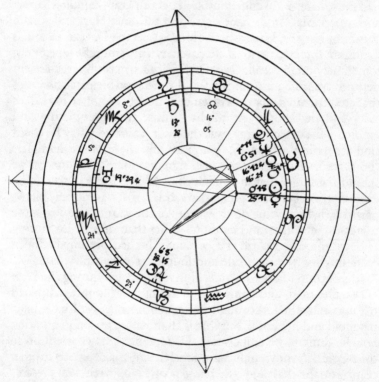

*Chart 22*
Adolf Hitler: 20 April 1889, 6.30pm LMT, Braunau, Austria (48N15, 13E03).

measure morality. Consequently, we easily drift into an assumption that harmonious aspects involving benefic planets make nice people. Jupiter is not a particularly moral planet; although I am sure many of us would like to have a stronger Jupiter in our charts, it is because we feel we would be happier or more successful, not because we feel it would make us better people. Jupiter bestows his benefits on just and unjust with equal generosity.

It is a favourite pastime among astrologers to dig into Hitler's chart seeking explanations for the horrors of the Third Reich, and I have little new to offer in explaining the man's brutality — the chart does not present itself as the chart of a monster. Mars/Saturn contacts have a nasty reputation of course; the Marquis de Sade, like Hitler, had the square, and Venus is involved in both cases, conjunct Saturn and square Mars in de Sade's case and conjunct Mars and square Saturn in Hitler's. Hard aspects from Saturn to Mars can be felt as a constant threat to personal effectiveness which must be repeatedly, sometimes brutally, challenged. On Mars much masculine self-esteem depends. Venus/Saturn tends to fear closeness and prefer relationships that are structured, kept at a distance or under control, so in Hitler's case (and de Sade's) one might surmise that dominating and enforcing his will on others was the most satisfactory way he could find of relating. Although Venus is technically stronger than Mars (both are in Taurus, Venus's own sign and Mars's detriment), we should not forget that in a man's chart Mars is likely to seek more expression, or that Hitler grew up in a society that traditionally placed particularly high value on the virtues of the warrior and was more repressive of women and feminine values than most. Also, during Hitler's unsuccessful career as a painter he had presumably been exercising his Venusian side and found it got him nowhere.

It is of course false to blame all that happened during the Nazi era on one man, and dangerous to assume that it only happened because a madman acquired power. Hitler may well have been paranoid and hysterical, but that is all the more reason to question how he came to be empowered. Liz Greene[10] draws attention to the Neptune/Pluto conjunction, which has no major aspects to other planets on the chart and is therefore poorly integrated, and presents Hitler as the carrier of collective energies, and this he undoubtedly was. In the light of this view it is interesting to look at the synastry between Hitler's chart and that for the proclamation of Wilhelm I as German Emperor, which Charles Carter[11] claims to have proven its validity as a chart for the unified German nation throughout two world wars. The only exact major interaspects are the conjunction between Hitler's Mars/Venus and Pluto on the Germany chart, and the opposition between Hitler's twelfth house Uranus and the Germany Neptune, so it is precisely through those two planets that we might expect the German people to have experienced him. The Germany Jupiter also aspects these points (semi-sextile Hitler's Venus/Mars and trine his Uranus).

Jupiter in Hitler's chart is in the third in Capricorn, conjunct the Moon, trine the Sun, and widely trine Venus and Mars. [12] Obviously there is greater ease in the Sun/Jupiter trine than in the square discussed above, but Jupiter in Capricorn has a degree of struggle in expressing itself, the expansive tendency needing to proceed in a measured, concrete, organized fashion. Hitler proclaimed the need for 'Lebensraum', i.e. the need for nations to expand physically (Jupiter and the planets it contacts are in *earth* signs) as one of the fundamental forces of history, and territorial expansion was a major Nazi policy, systematically pursued. For Hitler these imperial ambitions also meant personal aggrandizement.

The Moon/Jupiter conjunction is particularly interesting. The charts of all four Nazi leaders included in this chapter, who were involved from fairly early days until the collapse of the regime, have major aspects between the two planets. Moon/Jupiter is really a very emotional combination, generally open about and expressive of feelings, and easily swept away by them — think of Hitler wallowing in Wagner — and is undoubtedly helpful in stirring up public enthusiasm and hysteria. The placement of the Moon/Jupiter conjunction in Hitler's third house seems to me one of the keys to his success. The Neptune/Pluto conjunction highlighted by Liz Greene is in Gemini. The years when these two planets were within orb of conjunction saw major developments in the communication media with the invention of wireless and cinematography. Much of Hitler's success was due to the imaginative exploitation of the new media. Apart from the extensive use of radio broadcasting for propaganda, he also distributed gramophone records of his speeches to be played at meetings, and had films made both for propaganda purposes and as a record for future generations.

The very word *broadcasting* has a Jupiterian ring — the verb's first meaning is to sow seeds by spreading them round with circling movements of the hand, and presidents F. D. Roosevelt and Reagan have also shown a considerable gift for broadcast talks. Sowing seeds of course is also *propagation,* and the notion of propaganda, the spreading of persuasive 'information' could not be better expressed astrologically than by Jupiter in the third.

Without his oratorical ability, in which his forceful Mercury in Aries, conjunct an angle and electrified by the opposing Uranus also played a significant role, Hitler would have been nothing. The insignificant-looking little man was transformed when he opened his mouth to address a crowd. Films of his speeches demonstrate the Moon/Jupiter conjunction — high emotion, uttered in a controlled, in fact carefully calculated manner. Hitler rehearsed his speeches systematically, using photographers to record his use of different gestures at critical points so that he could select the most effective — the actor again. When this fact leaked out he was furious, as this spoiled the image that the use of such techniques was designed to create. He was extremely sensitive about his public image, as is indicated by his Saturn on the midheaven in Leo — the man who worked hard at being king, who desperately wanted public recognition and had failed to find it as a painter.

Given Hitler's strong Jupiter contacts and his effect on the German public, we should perhaps consider the concept of enthusiasm, a word mostly used with decidedly positive connotations and without which our lives would be duller and less creative. Enthusiasm originally meant 'possession by a god', and possession is an apt description of both Hitler himself in the act of making a speech, and of those who listened to him. Extreme enthusiasm is a condition in which one is taken over by something bigger than oneself, filled with overpoweringly positive feelings — a wonderful state to be in, divine, a state in which one's mortal limitations and frailty are eclipsed. As Firmicus — enthusiastic in his admiration for the qualities of Jupiter — suggests,[13] Jupiter can make us feel like gods, without limitations, and perhaps at the most extreme without humanity. Such uplifting emotions held all the more allure for a nation suffering not only economic depression but humiliating repression resulting from the Treaty of Versailles. Like Hefner, who banned the word 'no' from his presence, Hitler increasingly surrounded himself with yes-men and eventually came to shut out all depressing news from his world, dismissing or even executing critics and bearers of bad tidings, the better to persuade himself that he was immortal.

The Nazi Party produced two great orators, and both had Jupiter in the house of communication. In some ways Josef Goebbels, who became the chief propagandist for the party, and after it came to power became Reich Minister for Information and Propaganda, deserves greater opprobrium than his master, for Hitler at least seems to have believed in his policies. For Goebbels (Leo rising, Sun conjunct Mars in Scorpio) the only motives were power and devotion to the Fuehrer. He was not a racist, yet he was willing to promote racist policies of the most hideous kind. His political views were distinctly to the left, but these and other beliefs he suppressed in order to become Hitler's spokesman.

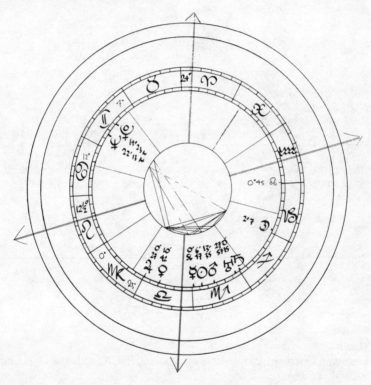

*Chart 23*
Josef Goebbels: 29 October 1897, 11.30pm MET, Rheydt, Germany (51N10, 6E27).

Hitler's Mercury is in Aries, Goebbels' in Mars's other sign, but more gently aspected, and the two benefics, Jupiter and Venus, are in Libra in the third. Like Hitler he rehearsed his speeches, and although Hitler could hold his audience spellbound like no other,

Goebbels was the more polished performer. He was the inventor of
the Big Lie. 'He talked of the integrity of the government, knowing
it was corrupt. He spoke of victory when defeat became
inevitable.'[14]. He was a superbly effective salesman and as such an
arch hypocrite.

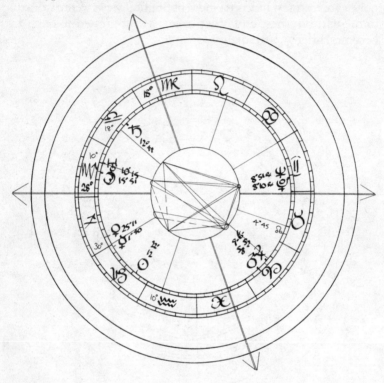

*Chart 24*
Hermann Goering: 12 January 1893, 4.00am MET, Rosenheim, Germany
(47N51, 12E06).

Of the top Nazis, the one who came nearest to what is generally
understood as the jovial type was Hermann Goering, the Reich
Marshall and Hitler's appointed successor, who had Jupiter square
the Sun, quincunx the Moon, widely trine Venus in Sagittarius,
conjunct Mars and opposition Saturn. Mars in Aries rules a Scorpio
ascendant and describes a man of passions and a fighter. The
conjunction with Jupiter, also in Aries, suggests one who fights

energetically for what he believes in, well-suited to the warrior religion of his forefathers, and with the fiery Jupiter on the cusp of the fifth and square the Sun, he carried himself with a certain amount of swagger, despite the Capricorn Sun.

He was a distinctly flamboyant character, with a love of art (Venus in the first) and the good life, and a sizeable wardrobe of uniforms, suits and sporting clothes, among which he loved to ring the changes. Generally likeable and certainly generous, he was a larger-than-life character, a leading minister who sat in a vast office behind a huge desk, like Hitler's, a heroic World War I fighter pilot and a man with wide-ranging interests and an extravagant lifestyle. In traditional Jupiterian style he put on a lot of weight after a slim beginning (he was a compulsive eater). He loved entertaining in his splendid hunting-lodge home (Jupiter conjuncts Mars in the fourth?).

The conjunction in Aries is opposed by Saturn. There is a struggle between the heroic/zealous/dashing and the controlling (the Sun is in Capricorn, too, and in wide square to Saturn), between belief in his own powers and a sense of his limitations. There is a great potential for frustration here, and great potential for overcoming frustration, and in a big way. This combination can be illustrated with an episode from his youth. Having joined up with the infantry he learned of the developments in wartime aviation and immediately scented an opportunity for glory. He applied for a transfer, but aware that time was short forged the transfer documents (the request was subsequently refused) and simply left his regiment to start training as a pilot. He got away with it — perhaps thanks to his good record and his sheer popularity. He had not been rebelling exactly; it was a blatant refusal to be bound by the rules, Mars/Jupiter refusing to acknowledge Saturn. Mostly Goering got away with it until 1945, though times of confident activity and exertion were sometimes paid for with periods of depression. Occasionally when frustrated, his violent temper would break out, in typical Mars/Saturn fashion, but he was not a cruel man.

The Sun/Jupiter/Mars/Saturn T-square has a very ambitious feeling about it, especially with Saturn in the tenth. It strains towards expansion, works hard to be first and greatest. Only Hitler was recognized by Goering as greater than himself, only from Hitler would he accept limitations. He was an appealing figure to a people who felt harshly constrained, nostalgic for greatness and hungry for more of the world's resources.

Of all the principal figures of the Third Reich, the one who enjoyed the most prominent Jupiter was Heinrich Himmler, the dreaded chief of the SS, yet he is the most impenetrable. One might expect from his chart, dominated as it is by a grand trine in fire, with Jupiter in Sagittarius right on the midheaven and conjunct Uranus, that he too would have been the flamboyant type, but not at all. Although some who knew him privately remarked on his 'vivacious personality' and 'capacity for enthusiasm',[15] he seems to have been rather

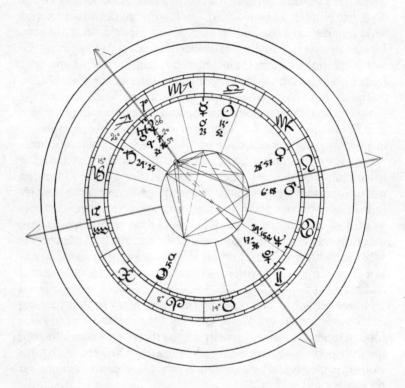

*Chart 25*
Heinrich Himmler: 7 October 1900, 3.30pm MET, Munich (48N08, 11E35).

introverted and generally came across as insignificant, mediocre even. 'But Himmler was not altogether mediocre. He possessed a fanatical vision and energy and an image of himself as a figure in power politics which made him in ten years one of the masters of Europe.'[16] His fieriness did not express itself in extravagant gestures, but as powerful fantasy and a burning sense of mission.

Someone remarked to me that the most striking feature of Himmler was his 'wierd beliefs', which is one good way of interpreting Jupiter conjunct Uranus, and those wierd beliefs inspired the development of the SS. Alen Oken says of this conjunction that the 'person often has original ideas and concepts which he or she enjoys sharing with others.' [17] Through a combination of opportunism and sheer good luck, Himmler rose rapidly to a position which enabled him to act out his fantasies. He modelled the brutal and elitist SS in part on the Teutonic Knights, one of the terrifying military-religious orders founded in the twelfth century, and began to see himself as the Grand Master of this new order.

It is all there in the chart, particularly in the grand trine. The aspects to Jupiter from Mars in Leo and the Moon in Aries contribute the martial, heroic aspect of his fantasy (though unlike Goering, Himmler was no hero in reality, but loved to wear the uniform of an Army Commander). There is also the wide opposition from ruthless Pluto, while the Uranus conjunction and Aquarian ascendant are attracted to ideas of brotherhood.

Jupiter rules the eleventh, and in that house is Saturn, co-ruler of the chart; Saturn in the eleventh can long to be a fully paid-up member of the club, while having difficulty in ever feeling accepted, and may find it easier to be part of something very formal and highly organized.

In July 1934, with his progressed Venus in exact sextile to that visionary Jupiter, he acquired his dream-house, the castle of Wewelsburg, in which he indulged in mock-mediaeval charades with selected SS officers, apparently fantasizing himself as a reincarnation of Heinrich I, the tenth-century founder of the German Reich. Jupiter conjunct the MC is not necessarily ambitious, but when it is it knows no bounds, and here Uranus adds a wilfulness and urgency. Of particular interest too is the lack of planets in earth signs to counteract the fiery imagination with a sense of plain matter-of-factness. As often happens where there is a lack of earth, Himmler compensated by developing an obsessive meticulousness in his work, but behind the pedantic bureaucrat was the man who saw himself as a king. In a less fraught environment such inflation might have been harmless, but it made it relatively easy for Himmler to exalt the German nation and his role in it, and to high-handedly dismiss the

Jewish race. In setting up the concentration camps he acted impersonally, at a distance, as suited his Aquarian ascendant, while, like the others, he was privately quite kind, fond of animals, even sentimental (Moon trine Jupiter and square Neptune).

He was in his way an essentially religious (or perhaps superstitious) man, who searched the sacred books of various religions for ideas which fitted his vision, to which alone he was faithful. 'He saw himself as a teacher and reformer, born to change the world.' [18] He loved preaching. Religion was a necessity for him, and he envisaged himself as playing a leading, even messianic, role in it — he has been quoted as saying that he longed to be Minister for Religious Affairs. 'I insist that members of the SS must believe in God. I'm not going to have men around me who refuse to recognize any higher being or Providence or whatever you like,' [19] he once declared. And that higher being, or whatever you like, was of course on Himmler's side, Germany's side. With such a sense of rightness and importance he could afford to think big. In announcing in an order, signed by himself, the opening of Dachau, which was to accommodate 5,000 prisoners, he commented: 'Planning on such a scale, we refused to be influenced by any petty objections, since we are convinced this will reassure all those who have regard for the nation and serve their interests.' [20] 'To the last he failed to understand why his name became so hated. He believed he was a good man who, if he made mistakes, had made them in good cause.' [21]

Nothing can bring to our attention more graphically than the Nazi regime the dangers of an unrestrained Jupiter. Hitler, with Jupiter in earth, sought material expansion, Himmler, with Jupiter in Sagittarius saw things more in spiritual than material terms. For Goering (Jupiter in Aries) the vision was one of glory, for Goebbels (Jupiter in Libra) something more detached. They all recognized an opportunity when they saw it, all identified with something immeasurably great. None of them felt the need to stop at any particular point. For much of their lives Jupiter was indeed benefic to them, though they owed something of their downfall to overextension and, in Hitler's case at any rate, overestimation of their ability and resources. The god did not abandon them until millions had been slaughtered. The people may indeed perish where there is no vision, but riding on an inspiring vision and swept along by a tide of enthusiasm they can be caught up by hideously destructive forces.

# Notes

1. Betty Lunsted: *Astrological Insights into Personality*, Astro Computing Services, San Diego, 1980.
2. Quoted in George Gardiner's *Margaret Thatcher*, William Kimber, London, 1975.
3. Shakespeare: *Henry V*, Act III, Scene I.
4. Graham Ellis: 'Astrology and the Philosophical Mind' in *Astrology*, summer & autumn 1983 (vol. 57 Nos. 2 & 3). The author analysed Sun/Jupiter and Mercury/Jupiter aspects on the charts of ninety philosophers and found both types of aspect scored significantly above chance, and in particular the conjunction, square, septile and decile.
5. Michel Gauquelin: *The Spheres of Destiny*, Corgi, 1981.
6. Michael Baigent:'The Astrological Chart of the United States', *Astrological Journal*, Winter 1980-81.
7. See, for example, Nicholas Culpeper's seventeenth-century writings on medical astrology, and Klibansky, Saxl and Panofsky: *Saturn and Melancholy*, Nelson, London, 1964.
8. Stephen Arroyo: *Relationships and Life Cycles*, CRCS, 1979, p. 88.
9. Quoted in *The Times*, 21 February 1975.
10. Liz Greene: *The Outer Planets and their Cycles*, CRCS, 1979.
11. Charles Carter: *An Introduction to Political Astrology*, Fowler, London, 1951, p. 31.
12. It is also undoubtedly of significance that Chiron opposes the Moon/Jupiter conjunction from 6°55′ Cancer, but too little is known about Chiron at this stage for me to venture an interpretation.
13. See note on p. 65.
14. Viktor Reimann: *Joseph Goebbels: The Man who Created Hitler*, Sphere Books, 1979, p. 241.
15. The Swedish Count Bernadotte on first meeting him. Quoted in R. Manvell & H. Fraenkel: *Heinrich Himmler*, Heinemann, 1965, p. 219.
16. Roger Manvell and Heinrich Fraenkel: *Heinrich Himmler*, Heinemann, 1965, p. 187.
17. *Alen Oken's Complete Astrology*, Bantam, 1980, p. 427. (Originally published in *The Horoscope, the Road and its Travellers*, 1974.)
18. Manvell and Fraenkel: *Heinrich Himmler*, Heinemann, 1965.

19. Ibid.
20. Ibid.
21. Ibid. p. 187.

**DATA**

| | |
|---|---|
| USA: | Michael Baigent in the *Astrological Journal*, Winter 1980-81. |
| F. D. Roosevelt: | Astrological Association Data Section. |
| Ronald Reagan: | Lois Rodden: *American Book of Charts*, Astro Computing Services, San Diego, 1980. Dirty Data. |
| Margaret Thatcher: | Astrological Association Data Section. |
| Adolf Hitler: | AA Data Section. |
| Josef Goebbels: | *American Book of Charts*. |
| Heinrich Himmler: | *American Book of Charts*. |

# 10.

# Crime

It has to be admitted, by those who have seriously studied the requisite number of cases, that Jupiter can very definitely incline to crime, and this, too, when in technical 'good' aspect.

Charles Carter[1]

After consideration of the Nazi charts it will surprise no one that Jupiter should come up in discussion on crime. I am taking Carter's word for it that Jupiter commonly figures in charts of criminals, but differ somewhat in my interpretation of this. Carter suggests that the 'motive is probably the need to repair the ravages of extravagance or the desire to procure the means for prodigal enjoyment, luxury or splendid living'. That may indeed be a motive at times, but in neither of the cases presented here was financial gain an issue. To the extent that Jupiter participates in crime I feel it is more particularly as a granter of licence and liberator from constraint. A strong Jupiter disinclines one to halt at the barriers set up by decree, encourages the feeling that one has a 'higher authority' than the letter of the law, and is an ally in 'getting away with it', or at least promotes the belief that one can do so.

The two mass murderers Denis Nilsen and Peter Sutcliffe were born just over six months apart, and their charts have a number of features in common. The main aspects between outer planets, apart from the Neptune/Pluto sextile which pertained for decades and is still with us at the time of writing, are Jupiter trine Uranus and Jupiter square Saturn. Then there is the Mars/Pluto conjunction in Leo, which is just over 10 degrees from exact on Sutcliffe's chart but may still have some effect. Both charts lack any emphasis on earth (unless Sutcliffe's midheaven is in Virgo). Both have Moon/Saturn conjunctions (squared by Jupiter). Nilsen has Venus in Scorpio, square Pluto, and Sutcliffe Venus in the eighth, semi-sextile Pluto. Both have strong Mercury/Uranus contacts, though this I feel is not directly relevant. Finally, both have strong Jupiters. In Sutcliffe's case he rules the chart (Sagittarius rising) and forms a major aspect with every planet except Neptune. Nilsen has Jupiter exactly conjunct the ascendant, and his Sun is in Sagittarius.

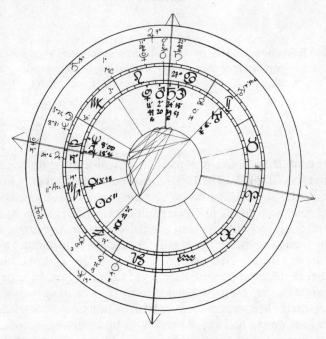

*Chart 26*
Denis Nilsen: 23 November 1945, 4.00am GMT, Fraserburgh
(57N41, 2W00).
Progressions for 31 December 1978 — First murder.

Denis Nilsen was arrested on 9 February 1983 after men who had been called to investigate blocked drains in the house where he lodged discovered human remains, which had been hacked up and disposed of in the lavatory. He confessed to fifteen murders of young men over a period of four years, only two of whom had even been reported as missing — the remains of the rest were found later. Already one may like to see the hand of Jupiter at work. How could it have been so easy and attracted no suspicion? He was a civil servant, remarkable only for his trade union activities which irritated his superiors and blocked his way to promotion. I understand[2] that Sagittarius is a favourite sign for union leaders; though not necessarily rebellious, it is a sign that believes in freedom and does not take easily to being bossed, and is usually good at stirring interest in others.

With Libra rising, the issue of friends (or enemies) and partners looms large, the need to have another person around as a counterweight, to share ideas, provide another point of view. Sagittarius and Libra are both generally sociable signs. But Venus, ruler of Libra and of the chart, is in Scorpio and squared by Pluto. With such a combination relationships are not going to be as light and civilized as Libra would have them, but involve a trip to the underworld or a struggle for power. Venus/Pluto people need to relate deeply and can experience intense loneliness. Jupiter rising generally rejoices in a feeling of 'going somewhere' and appears confident (he often did), but here of course it is engaged in a lifelong struggle with Saturn. Mars, ruler of the seventh, is conjunct Pluto, so that dark lord (or is she a mistress?) comes up again in the relationship context. Mars/Pluto is definitely violent on some level, though of course this need not be acted out literally, and Mars being conjunct the MC brings this more firmly into focus. The fact that Mars, in lordly Leo, also conjuncts Saturn is likely to aggravate any tendency to violence, through frustration, rather than reduce it. There is also implicit in this Pluto/Mars/Saturn combination the possibility of strong but frustrated sexual urges. Nilsen was a lonely man who longed for a lasting relationship but was incapable of forming one, partly because he was shy (Moon conjunct Saturn), partly because his inclinations were homosexual and his strict upbringing had made it difficult for him to acknowledge this openly.

He had had a difficult start in life, his father, having scarcely been around at all, being divorced by his mother when Nilsen was 3. She was too busy struggling to survive to devote much time to him, hence the unloved feel of Moon/Saturn. Does the Mars/Pluto conjunction in the tenth also reflect something violent connected with his mother? A case could certainly be made for interpreting the tenth here as the father, or the grandfather who was a father-substitute for some years. His mother's father was the person dearest to him, and when the latter died at sea and was laid out in a room in the family home, the 6-year-old was carried in to see the corpse without any mention of death. The impression made by the pale, still body of his favourite person was both profound and puzzling. Neptune was conjunct his ascendant: a time of mystery and uncertainty. It took him a long time to understand what had happened, and he clung to this last image of his grandfather. His Scorpio Venus, which also rules the eighth, was trined by Uranus at the time of the death; it had moved on from the natal quincunx. It was a relationship abruptly ended, a shocking experience, and the beginning of a confusion in which love and death were to become hopelessly embroiled. Pluto at this time was also in trine to his Mercury, ruler of the ninth and eleventh. One can surmise that his outlook on life was profoundly affected and wonder about the effect on his capacity to join in with others. He was certainly unable to communicate about or make sense of the situation.

This story of a child's loss and confusion provides a clue to understanding his later fantasies about death and eventual necrophilia, and these are chillingly symbolized by the Pluto aspects to Venus and Mars. The title given to the excellent biography of Nilsen by Brian Masters is also fitting: *Killing for Company*.[3] Longing to get close to people, Nilsen could only relate to corpses: he even sat them in chairs, duly washed and dressed, to watch television with him.

Fantasy is one thing, murder another. It is easy to see the fantasist in the chart, with Neptune and possibly Jupiter in the twelfth house and a complete lack of earth. How did the fantasy come to be acted out? The transits and progressions at the time of his initiation into murder are revealing. The principal progressions are the trine of Mercury to Pluto, the square of the ascendant to Pluto (the sort of thing one might expect) and the quincunx of Saturn to Venus. Transiting Saturn is additionally in sextile to Venus. Nilsen had just been rejected yet again by someone he hoped would share his lonely life with him. By transit, Neptune is at 19 Sagittarius, Uranus at 20 Scorpio, Pluto at 19 Libra, all picking out the natal square between Jupiter, ascendant and Moon. The Moon rules the midheaven, and in his career Nilsen had also received a blow — his expected promotion had been denied him. Moon/Jupiter is a volatile combination, and one can imagine extremes of emotion, generally held in check by Saturn, breaking out at this time. He could not stop himself from feeling. The passage of Pluto over the ascendant is always a major transition, an experience of death on some level, or of violence being done to one, and here Pluto is also conjunct Jupiter. Any transits to Jupiter can make us shift our perspective, modify our outlook or world view, and Pluto transits to Jupiter can darken our hopes, force us to seek meaning in darkness, or deep within ourselves. Pluto also intensifies, and can make us burningly aware of our frustrations, leading to explosions. There is much kindness and goodwill in Moon/Jupiter, but now it had nowhere to go. Perhaps, under the cloak of Pluto it enabled Nilsen to convince himself that in strangling a young man he had picked up and brought home he was doing good to another lonely, unwanted, hopeless individual, a sentiment he was to express in poems to some of his dead victims. Of course there must also have been the experience of power — strangulation gives prolonged power of life and death over the victim — and this time he had arranged things so his lover could not leave him.

The role of Jupiter has to do with release from inhibition — Nilsen usually drank quite heavily before committing his murders, and I think alcohol can put inhibited people more in touch with their Jupiter. Jupiter/Uranus is particularly eager to go beyond all restraint, but the square from Saturn blocks and taunts that Jupiterian expectation of unlimited freedom to grow, setting up a struggle between freedom and control, so that the individual may feel compelled to resist that control and prove himself a free agent — as Goering did when abandoning his regiment. Nilsen was stuck, he was not allowed to move on and grow, so he found his own Plutonian way of doing it. Transiting Jupiter was on the midpoint of his Mars/Pluto conjunction: a new possibility for exercising his power opened up, a new kind of relationship (Mars rules the seventh) and sexuality.

Peter Sutcliffe, the Yorkshire Ripper, suffered like Nilsen from cramping of the feelings (Moon/Saturn) and shyness, except on the rare occasions when he got drunk and became over-excited (Moon/Jupiter). He was secretive, a loner, with a private fantasy life (Neptune trine Sun, conjunct the midheaven) which sometimes took gruesome forms. He was also obsessed with death (five planets, including Mars and Pluto, in the eighth, and Sun sextile Pluto). He worked as a gravedigger in his late teens, and relished the work. The Sun in the seventh suggests that he needed to find himself through relationships, but he could not get really close to people. He also

felt less than adequate sexually (Saturn in the eighth?) and felt
mocked by women. It is speculated that what tipped him over into
murder was the fact that his idealized mother (Neptune in the tenth)
had an affair, two or three years before the killing started. The exact
Moon/Saturn conjunction suggests that though he may have had

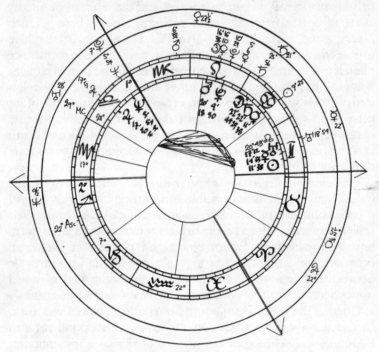

*Chart 27*
Peter Sutcliffe: 2 June 1946, 8.30pm BST, Bingley (53N51, 1W50).
Progressions for 5 July 1975 — First murder attempt.

positive feelings towards his mother he did not feel truly nurtured
by her. Whatever ambivalent feelings he may have had with respect
to her, he certainly divided women into good and bad, and eventually
set out to destroy the bad women, particularly prostitutes, because
they had not helped him to find his manhood. He had killed and
mutilated thirteen women before he was caught, having repeatedly
slipped through the net of police enquiries.
   'It was a miracle they didn't apprehend me earlier . . . They had
all the facts for a long time, but then I knew why they didn't catch

me. Everything was in God's hands.'[4] These words were spoken by Sutcliffe during the trial, in the course of which he also spoke of voices from God which urged him to kill. Much was made of this 'divine mission' story, and although it may have been concocted to produce a verdict of insane it does emphasize that taking another person's life into one's hands is playing a 'quasi-God role' (words used by Nilsen). Perhaps it is not fanciful to imagine that killing can make a man feel not only powerful but free, for he has gone beyond all the normal bounds. Sutcliffe earlier in his life had got considerable pleasure out of a blithe disregard for the rules, by, for example, regularly driving a car without licence, tax or insurance. Once he even went to the police for assistance when he ran out of petrol on an illegal jaunt. With Sagittarius rising and Sun trine Jupiter one might expect a casual attitude to such formalities, but I feel that the square from Saturn made it important to prove the point, to push his luck.

Sutcliffe made his first murder attempt at the time of his Saturn return, with progressed Sun semi-sextile Pluto. The progressed descendant was also conjunct the Moon/Saturn conjunction, if the birth time is correct, and Jupiter was in square to it, forming a rough T-square with the natal Moon/Jupiter square. As with Nilsen, he must have been going through a difficult time, during which he would have re-experienced the past hurts implied by that chilled Moon, a familiar encounter with rejection, very likely from a woman. When the Jupiter transit came along he went overboard, his feelings had to have an outlet, though even then they were controlled enough to permit a certain amount of planning.

Some may claim that Jupiter played no part in the Sutcliffe murders, but it must at least be asked how the 'protective' influence of such a strong Jupiter did not prevent such deeds. This cannot be the planet of which it has been written: 'The real character of Jupiter is good nature, freedom, and a conscious confidence, openness, and a disposition that would feel a difficulty in doing or contriving to do wrong, and could never, under any circumstances, be a bad character.'[5]

## Notes

1.  Charles Carter: *Essays on the Foundations of Astrology,* Theosophical Publishing House, 1978, p. 33 (orig. edn 1947).
2.  From Charles Harvey.

3.  Brian Masters: *Killing for Company*, Jonathan Cape, 1985.
4.  Gordon Burn: . . . *Somebody's Husband, Somebody's Son*, Pan, 1985, p. 326 (first pubd by Heinemann, 1984).
5.  James Wilson: *A Complete Dictionary of Astrology*, Samuel Weiser, New York, 1969, p. 313 (orig. edn 1819).

# 11.
# Law

Law and the legal profession are traditionally assigned to Jupiter, but the word 'law' has numerous applications, many of which seem unrelated to the planet. Charles Carter[1] was sufficiently puzzled about the connection to ask: 'Is the attribution not merely overstressed, but actually faulty?'. I have not got an answer to the question. There are certainly some connections to be made between our planet and law, but they do not add up to a particularly clear picture. I note also that William Lilly, whose work is almost scriptural to many horary astrologers, does not list legal matters under the ninth house: law suits he ascribes to the seventh, and lawyers to the tenth.[2] The Oxford English Dictionary traces the word *law* back to an Old Icelandic term meaning 'something laid or fixed', which is more suggestive of Saturn, but later includes a section on *divine law*, and it is here, I believe, that we get nearer to the association with Jupiter: 'The body of commandments which express the will of God with regard to the conduct of His intelligent creatures'.

To the Greeks, at least in the earlier days of Zeus's reign, at the time of the *Iliad*, the king of the gods stood not for morality but for the maintenance of order. The Greek concept of *Dike* or justice (the goddess of that name became Zeus's daughter and sat beside his throne) had different connotations at different times, but basically meant correct or appropriate action and awareness of one's station.[3] The unforgivable human error, from Zeus's point of view, was hubris, that is to say the arrogation of properties belonging to the gods, going beyond the given limitations of one's station. Paradoxically, such inflationary transgressions are themselves characteristic of the astrological Jupiter.

The children of Jupiter are also sometimes inclined to 'lay down

the law' as if with divine authority, and their ability to convince
themselves and others of the rightness of their dogmatic statements
could serve them well in court. I do not have adequate material to
generalize on the relative prominence of Jupiter in charts of members
of the legal profession, but the planet has featured strongly in most
of the charts of barristers I have seen. This brings up the whole issue
of the dubious nature of Jupiterian morality, for a counsel must make
a plausible and persuasive case for his client regardless of personal
beliefs, and on the other hand we often hear of cases where a judge
oversteps the proper limits of his position and directs the jury towards
a decision in line with his personal views. Again it is a god-like
position. One may question whether Solomon's famous judgment
on the disputed baby, for all its 'wisdom', was truly moral.

A slightly more frivolous point worth mentioning is the 'dignity
of the law' as exemplified by the ritualistic element which slides easily
into pomposity, the banging of the gavel, the wigs, gowns and
neckgear. The bar, like the church, stage and military professions
involves an element of dressing up, something that has been
highlighted before in this book.

Perhaps we should also bear in mind that the legal profession as
a ninth house issue comes out of the more general background of
university education, which in turn developed under the auspices
of the Church. Although the letter of the law, which sets distinct
boundaries to what we may do, is Saturnian, the question of
interpretation leads us into the realm of speculation. A barrister
whom I questioned on this subject (she has the Sun in Gemini trined
by Jupiter, and three planets in Gemini in the ninth house, seemingly
an excellent qualification — Mercurial facility is clearly also vital in
an advocate) said that one of the most important qualities needed
was the ability to see a few moves ahead, to sniff out the possibilities,
spot the significant points and see where they led, which sounds
very Jupiterian. A certain toughness is also required, and must come
from some other astrological department, but a bit of acting ability
does not come amiss in hearings before a jury.

We have come back again to the ability to think speculatively:
if things go this way, this will be needed, if that way, something else
. . . A court of law always involves a speculative element, for however
good a case an individual may have there can be no sure prediction
of the outcome. This is the reason for the popularity of the television
courtroom drama, and for that matter the format of broadcast

debates, which owe a good deal of their appeal to the excitement of an uncertain outcome, as is the case in games of chance. To go to law always involves a gamble. There seems to be no end to the possibilities for finding a new way through the written statutes. Were the law entirely Saturnian there would be no need for hearings or advocates as the outcome would be a foregone conclusion.

Legal operations aside, Jupiter tends to draw us to the moral realm. In the end, although moral dilemmas are deeply personal, the notion of right and wrong rests on impersonal principles. Behind the Saturnian letter of the law, the laying down of legislative boundaries, and behind even the Libran concern of arriving at a just decision between opposing parties, stands this question of right and wrong which varies from individual to individual and from generation to generation, but always points beyond the immediate situation to moral generalization. The search for such underlying ethical principles is one of the functions of philosophy.

## Notes

1. Charles Carter: *Essays on the Foundations of Astrology*, Theosophical Publishing House, London, 1978, p. 32 (orig. edn 1947).
2. Williams Lilly: *Christian Astrology*, Regulus, London, 1985, pp. 54, 55 (orig. edn 1659).
3. Hugh Lloyd-Jones: *The Justice of Zeus*, University of California Press, 1972.

# 12.
# Theory

The ninth house is the house of physical travel, of flights of the spirit and of speculative thought, a house whose resources are mobilized to push out beyond the obvious and familiar with a view to gaining perspective on ourselves in relation to the world or cosmos at large. To speculate, a Jupiterian word in more than one of its senses, comes from the word for a watchtower (Latin *specula*), a high place from which one can look out in all directions, enjoy a broad view, see things from a distance. (I am reminded of the academic's well-known 'ivory tower'.) Speculations on the nature of things are expressed in theories (ways of looking or viewing, from the same root as *theatre*, a place where spectacles are viewed.) 'Thus it might be said that theory is primarily a form of *insight*, i.e. a way of looking at the world, and not a form of *knowledge* of how the world is.'[1] Jupiter's domain is not reducible to Saturnian facts. Theories represent our attempts to arrive at underlying laws, and their development is one of the principal tasks of universities.

Jupiter and the ninth house relate to all such speculation and theorizing, but particularly to philosophy, which perhaps reaches out farther into the unknown than other disciplines, and should enable us to rise above petty concerns. Its aim according to Ludwig Wittgenstein is to 'show the fly the way out of the fly bottle', to liberate from Saturnian confines. Graham Ellis in his research into aspects found certain of the Sun/Jupiter and Mercury/Jupiter contacts considerably more common in the charts of philosophers than those of other academics (see note on page 119). The conjunction and square, and also the septile and decile, were particularly significant in the cases of both types of aspect, the trine only at chance level and the opposition below chance, suggesting that the desire to explore in this fashion is experienced with great urgency only in certain harmonics.

As philosophers must have a particularly strong attunement to the Jupiterian dimension, further study of Jupiter on philosophers' charts would probably be instructive, and Jupiter's position and aspects may have some bearing on the nature of their theories. The Jupiter sign tells us how a person sets about exploring or speculating, and I have been struck by how often Jupiter's element in philosophers' charts seems to be relevant. Jupiter in fire signs tends to emphasize spirit, transcendence and faith at the expense of involvement with the material world (e.g. Kierkegaard, Hegel, and even Descartes), while Jupiter in earth seems more inclined towards here-and-now reality. Spinoza (Sun in Sagittarius, Jupiter in Taurus) begins his *Ethica* with a definition of substance, and finds Descartes' belief in a transcendent deity offensive. Sartre, one of whose basic tenets is that 'existence precedes essence' (earth before fire?) also has Jupiter in Taurus, while empiricist John Stuart Mill, who referred to himself as a 'Utilitarian', has Jupiter in Capricorn. Marx also has Jupiter in this sign, and it falls in the eleventh house, trining Sun and Moon in Taurus in the second, which seems an appropriate position by house as well as by element (collectivism, materialism). Most philosophy claims to be based on reason, which is perhaps an airy concept, and I am not too clear about Jupiter-in-air philosophers, except that I would expect a detached and sceptical approach. Kant falls into this category, and so does Einstein (Jupiter in Aquarius), who showed an exceptional willingness to be proven wrong in the name of truth. I also note Jung's Jupiter in Libra in relation both to his emphasis on thinking to counteract the dangers of blind faith (of course he also has Aquarius rising) and the principle of opposites and enantiodromia which are fundamental to his thought. I have found very few major philosophers with Jupiter in water signs — perhaps this placement tends more to the contemplative. Nietzsche has Jupiter in Pisces; the book which made his reputation as a thinker was *The Birth of Tragedy,* in which he argues that the spirit of rationalism, exemplified in Socrates, brought about the death of tragedy, and argues for the restoration of the Dionysian element in art. He envisages the appearance of an artistic Socrates with a passion for poetry and music, and the Piscean preoccupation with suffering permeates his work. Liz Greene has pointed out the connection between Dionysos, whose story has strong connections with the

Christian myth, and the planet Neptune.

One cannot of course reduce the whole of a philosopher's complex thought to something so simple as Jupiter's sign, and to the extent that it is possible to find a thinker's preoccupations in his or her chart other factors must come into play, the nature of the ninth house, for example, and perhaps in particular the Sun, but further exploration of philosophers' Jupiter is surely merited.

## Notes
1. David Bohm: *Wholeness and the Implicate Order,* Routledge & Kegan Paul, 1980, p. 4.

# 13.

# Luck

Un coup de dès n'abolira jamais le hasard.

Mallarmé

We are prone to attribute good fortune to those who are successful in life ('You're so lucky to have a boat like this') when often we are envying the product of hard work, and this has little to do with Jupiter. In fact I do not think that Jupiter is to be associated directly with material prosperity — he is anything but an earthy planet — though indirectly he can be a great help in attaining it. A positive attitude to life tends to attract a positive response, and whether we attribute such a disposition to good parenting, good karma from past lives or the luck of the draw it is a Jupiterian quality. Not only is it possible to attract good things to oneself through 'positive thinking' or 'prosperity consciousness' (the sort of thing people with strong but not altogether well-aspected Jupiters tend to talk about) but the ability to see the possibilities and opportunities inherent in a situation is invaluable. Moreover the individual who looks on the bright side (the traditional sanguine temperament), is fortunately endowed even though he or she may have a difficult life in objective terms and even be materially poor.

(Good) luck is the secular equivalent to divine grace, and many people with a strong Jupiter report a feeling of special protection, and this I feel cannot entirely be put down to their own trust in providence. There certainly do seem to be people who have more than their fair share of luck, and David Livingstone's narrow escapes in the jungle, and in particular his discovery by Stanley when at the end of his tether — and when his Sun/Jupiter/Uranus grand trine was subject to a Jupiter transit (see page 60) transcend the possibilities of good management or temperament.

In the few cases of big wins in lotteries and the like I have been able to study, Jupiter has in the majority of cases not been especially strong or well aspected. Transits and progressions involving Jupiter do play a part, but more important is the eighth house, which governs property to which we do not have undisputed title. Perhaps there is a suggestion here not only of unearned bounty but of the strain such wins can impose on relationships. Out of six charts (five of which are those given by Lois Rodden in the *American Book of Charts*), four had Saturn transiting through the eighth at the time of the win, and three Venus, both planets with earthy connotations. None had Jupiter moving through the eighth, though one, who won during a once-in-a-lifetime gambling spree, had transiting Jupiter in the fifth.

Jupiter is notorious for encouraging people to rely too much on luck, in short to gamble, and gambling seems to be common to all cultures and an important element in games and sports (the principal sense in which sport is a Jupiterian activity, I feel). Gambling appears to have its origin in divination,[1] by which means we can see more than ordinary modes of perception allow, particularly things which lie in the future. Jupiter is of course associated with this kind of seeing and also rules the liver, the organ most commonly used for divination by the ancients. The purpose of such an exercise was to compel the god to reveal things the enquirer could turn to advantage, and by making offerings one could hope to coax the god over to one's side and receive a propitious answer. The purpose of gambling also seems to be to win some god over to one's side — or else to 'offer a challenge to fate', as Dostoevsky (a compulsive gambler himself) puts it in *The Gambler.*[2] The gambler, like the *haruspex* tends to develop rituals with which to approach the operation. Related to divination is Jung's concept of synchronicity, the coincidence of events connected in meaning but not in causal terms. This is surely also a Jupiterian phenomenon.

Research conducted among members of Gamblers Anonymous[3] confirms distinctly Jupiterian traits in compulsive gamblers. They regard material values with contempt. When they have money they are prodigal. They have 'fantasies of grandeur' and of 'disbursing bounty and charity'. They cease to value something when they have it in their grasp, preferring the hunt to the capture. But they also have traits strongly suggestive of Jupiterian/Saturn contacts: their state of mind 'alternates between hope and despair' and it is unclear whether in the end they want to win more than they feel compelled to lose. The whole idea of testing one's luck (or God's favour) smacks in fact of Jupiter/Saturn, and I suspect that hard aspects between the two would be found in the charts of a high proportion of compulsive gamblers. Liz Greene mentions the Jupiter/Saturn type 'who is . . . forever expecting the big break through some flash of good luck which somehow never comes'.[4] Dostoevsky has a close conjunction of the two planets in Aries, with a trine to Mars and quincunx to the Sun. The virtues of Saturn are of course needed to counteract the vices of Jupiter; Joyce Wehrman in her book on astrological gambling[5] stresses that while Jupiter encourages us to gamble, a strong Saturn is a must for the successful gambler. But a difficult contact *between* the two planets (and I wonder if any of them is altogether easy), especially when Jupiter is otherwise emphasized, can push the individual into a desperate struggle to prove him- or herself lucky or to entrap the god with an infallible system. Saturn seeks to imprison Jupiter, and Jupiter eludes and overpowers Saturn.

Speculation and the urge to nudge fate or destiny into action are evidently pretty basic urges and feature quite importantly in cosmological myths. In the *Iliad* (Book XV) Poseidon tells Iris how he, Zeus and Hades cast lots for the territories of sea, sky and underworld (the earth they kept in common). And: 'A famous saying of the philosopher Heraclitus is that Aion (the *durée creatrice,* the eternal, creative, divine Time, which is what Aion means in Greek) is a boy who . . . gambles on a board game.'[6] Einstein expressed his difficulty — on some other than rational level, as I understand it — in accepting quantum theory because he could not accept that God played dice with the universe; with quantum theory we have come back to the idea that at the root of things is a dice game, that there is nothing solid or certain but only probability, as if that were the ultimate law. Perhaps Jupiter is the planet of probability.

**Notes**

1. John Cohen: *Psychological Probability,* George Allen & Unwin, 1972, p. 85 and note.
2. Ibid. p. 66.
3. Ibid. p. 68ff.

4. Liz Greene: *Saturn,* Samuel Weiser, 1976 (Aquarian Press, 1977), p. 124.
5. Joyce Wehrman: *Winning,* published privately in California, 1980.
6. Marie-Louise Van Franz: *Divination and Synchronicity,* Inner City Books, Toronto, 1980, p. 58.

## Cookbook Section

It is hoped that the interpretations offered in this section, which can in many cases be illustrated by charts discussed earlier in the book, will stimulate readers to pursue their own interpretations; they are not intended to be exhaustive.

Jupiter's position by *sign*, modified by any aspects to him, describes the means we use to reach out to know or have what is beyond the immediate situation, to see higher orders of things, general laws and future possibilities. We open up new prospects and seek answers, for example, meticulously and in tangible, practical ways with Jupiter in Virgo, carelessly, extravagantly, riotously when he is in Sagittarius, subtly and intuitively in Pisces, crisply and coolly in Aquarius. The Jupiter sign can also be observed in the manner in which people express their views.

# 14.
# Jupiter in the Houses

**Jupiter in the First House**
With Jupiter in the first house there is an openness to the world around which others readily experience as welcoming. The dislike of those with this placement of restricting their options usually means that they are accessible to all classes of people. Similarly they tend to have a wide range of interests and show a willingness to try anything new and are often good at persuading others to join them.

There tends to be something of a happy-go-lucky approach to life, an expectation, usually justified, that as one door closes another will open, and they can often be seen to move through a number of successive lifestyles without effort, positively enjoying an element of risk and uncertainty in their lives in preference to predictable security. Punctuality is not a strong point, and this seems to rest both on a dislike of being bound by clock time and a trust that things will happen at the right time if allowed to do so.

Underlying this attitude is a trust in some sort of purpose beyond the power of human calculation, and this often amounts to or becomes a strong religious faith. Particularly in later life, and where there are difficult aspects this can lead to a rather dogmatic and even pompous style, which goes with a tendency to stand on one's own dignity, and this is more noticeable in the case of men. Those with this placement, however, usually have the saving grace of being able to laugh at themselves, and even if they hold to rigid views are open in other areas.

There is often a high appreciation of fun, and an ability to see the comic potential in a situation. The extreme example of this is the clown, who often started out using his or her ability to make people laugh as a way of easing anxiety, and here again challenging aspects to Jupiter tend to predominate. It is Jove at work convincing others that all is bright and sunny and gaining confidence from the positive feedback. Needless to say, the problem that this can lead to is that one becomes typecast as the buffoon, and the more complex feelings behind the mask never get an airing.

## Jupiter in the Second House

Jupiter is not particularly orientated towards material things except when he is in earth signs. Possessions restrict mobility and freedom and Jupiter in the second wants to be free of concern in these areas. There is often a carelessness with possessions and money, and a willingness to part with these in the expectation that material needs will be somehow provided for. The generosity that so often accompanies this placement tends to ensure that this faith is rewarded. Noel Coward's chart has a second house Jupiter and exemplifies this point well. Well-known for his extravagant lifestyle and openhanded-ness, there were times in his early career when he was very short of resources, but he never lacked friends to see him through hard times. One does however occasionally come across cases where improvidence and prodigality prove disastrous. Mozart was always ready to give or lend money to those in need, regardless of whether or not he could afford it, and he himself died in miserable poverty.

Sometimes Jupiter's gambling tendencies come out with this placement, and the desire to get beyond material problems without too much effort leads to foolish money-making schemes or speculations, but even if these ventures prove successful the resulting bounty does not usually last very long.

This position is probably most productive in financial terms when Jupiter is in an earth sign, so that it is through material substance that the individual sees the way forward to greater freedom and potential; there tends to be greater caution, in fact Jupiter in Taurus seems to be exceptionally good for business. Margaret Thatcher (see chart on page 107), who has Jupiter in the second in Capricorn, is a good example of someone with an economic vision. Her fervent belief in monetarism as the route to material expansion was based on faith in hard currency.

A fascinating tale of second house Jupiter is told by the case of Guy and Edna Ballard, whose charts have this position in common. In 1916 they founded a religious cult known as the 'Mighty I Am' movement, the fundamental tenet of which was that one must give in order to receive. The huge sums of money that poured in from donations eventually involved a criminal lawsuit. One can but speculate on the couple's motives: was it a wild and fraudulent business idea that paid off, or were they seeking the ultimate proof of God's existence manifested in the material world, true believers in the principle of casting one's bread upon the waters?

## Jupiter in the Third House

The third house represents the busy network of information exchange through learning, teaching, writing, and speech. Those with Jupiter in this house have a considerable appetite for collecting data from far-flung sources so as to arrive at general conclusions, and tend to be less interested in facts than in the speculations these lead to. Children with this placement usually enjoy the opportunity offered by schooling to exercise their enquiring minds even though they may lack the discipline of sticking to the curriculum. As with Jupiter/Mercury contacts words themselves may be a means of exploration and there is frequently an ability to convey more than the literal meaning of words through the use of symbolism.

With a mutable planet in a mutable house there is little desire to hang onto knowledge, and it is a good position for spreading the word. Many broadcasters have Jupiter in the third. Not only are they able in this way to reach out to a wider audience but often there is marked interviewing ability, that is to say a knack of asking the sort of question which opens up discussion or leads to significant issues. A third house Jupiter is also common among writers.

The examples of Martin Luther (chart on page 74) and Mrs Pankhurst demonstrate the flair of third house Jupiter for getting across a message, and the most sinister development of this potential can be seen in Hitler (page 109) and Goebbels (page 113) the chief Nazi propagandist, both of whom made brilliant use of the mass media. Sincerity is not a necessity for effectiveness in the promotion of ideas, and in any case it is easy to cross the delicate line between persuasiveness and untruth when Jupiter holds forth; to Jupiter literal truth is not necessarily the point. A third house Jupiter can be very helpful in selling or public relations but, particularly with a little help from Neptune, can make a convincing liar, trapped by the impressive sound of his or her own words.

## Jupiter in the Fourth House

While the midheaven may be said to represent a peak of conscious striving, the face we present to the public — and indeed quite often identify with — the IC has to do with those private depths we may fall back into if consciousness is diminished, a pool of early experiences often partly hidden even from ourselves. It refers to the fundamental sense of belonging — or lack of it — which forms the base on which our conscious structures are built. Those with Jupiter in this house may not have been born with a silver spoon in their mouths, but there has usually been a feeling of promise around them in their early days so that they are not later limited by narrow expectations of themselves.

Although the parent logically to be associated with this house would be the mother, and I am willing to accept that this may sometimes be the better interpretation, my experience generally confirms the traditional view that this is the house of the father. With Jupiter here there is generally a father or father-figure who conveys to the child something of the breadth of the world and encourages exploration ('he broadened my horizons' said one client), and although he may have exhibited some of Jupiter's worst characteristics — unreliable or somewhat tyrannical — he is usually remembered with gratitude.

Home is not usually felt by those with this placement to be a narrow retreat or cosy nest; the opposite extreme of keeping open house is more common, a liking for company to enliven the situation. In one of his roles Zeus was the protector of host and guest, and his hospitable side can be seen here particularly; in most cases this was a feature of the childhood home which is carried over into later life.

Planets in the fourth have a way of popping up unexpectedly, without conscious control, and Jupiter here is prone to emerging as a spontaneous sense of fun which comes to the rescue in situations that would otherwise be tricky.

## Jupiter in the Fifth House

The serious business described by the earthy houses: acquiring, ordering and achieving on the material plane, could scarely be effectively accomplished without the complementary creative impulse of fire, which precedes earth in the zodiacal cycle. Before work (sixth house) comes play,[1] and it must be the Protestant work ethic that would place such activity under the belittling heading of 'hobbies'. I would say rather that this house reflects our capacity to express ourselves by doing what we want to do rather than what we must.

Animals, even when fully grown, find time to play, which suggests that play fulfils a very basic need; in fact it is relatively easy to relate to other species on this level. A child at play tries out the range of life's possibilities, and the ability to play keeps adults elastic and creative.

With Jupiter in the fifth there is usually plenty of appetite and enthusiasm for fun and games, as much or more so than when he is in the first. There is usually a great love of pleasure, and though those with this placement are sometimes accused of self-indulgence they are happy to share their indulgence and are often highly entertaining.

There is often a distinctly exhibitionist streak. Jupiter's penchant for dressing up here seems to pick up something of Leo's liking for being on the stage, and this is a very popular position in the charts of actors and performers, a few examples being Marlene Dietrich, Peter Sellers, Janis Joplin, Bob Dylan, Bruce Lee, Raquel Welch and Vanessa Redgrave. Frequent love affairs seem to go with this position too, as an expression of an irrepressible urge to find ever more ways of having fun.

## Jupiter in the Sixth House

From Virgo's point of view, the ideal working day would be ordered yet flexible, co-ordinating the numerous necessary tasks as smoothly as possible for minimum effort and maximum efficiency, each item on the agenda having its place in a quasi-organic system. There would be very little chance of things getting out of control. Those with Jupiter in the sixth house are likely to feel imprisoned in such a highly organized world. There is impatience with routine, a preference for working according to the inspiration of the moment without such irksome restrictions as clocking in and out. There is a need to feel that the daily round points to something beyond itself, that there is scope for new discovery in it. Sixth house planets have a way of manifesting in those we work with, and Jupiter here often brings people in touch with colleagues who enliven the routine day and open doors to new experiences.

To synthesize Jupiter's vision with sixth house ordinariness is not particularly easy, and perhaps requires something of a Zen approach, according to which nothing is more significant than the trivial round of ordinary life, from cleaning teeth to filing papers. An element of ritual can be helpful; whereas Virgo creates rituals to keep chaos at bay, Jupiter develops rituals aimed at bringing the divine into manifestation.

The routine operations of the physical body are also a sixth house concern; we might say that ultimately this house has to do with an inner sense of order. Jupiter here seems to incline towards an intuitive and sometimes even spiritual approach to health and healing, and turns up often in the charts of holistic practitioners.

## Jupiter in the Seventh House

The notion that this is a fortunate position for marriage does not in my experience hold very much water; Jupiter here seems if anything less stable than Uranus; the institution of marriage is ill-equipped to satisfy Jupiter's insatiable appetite for new experience. How a person handles this placement will depend greatly on whether the implied restlessness is acknowledged as a part of him- or herself or whether it is always seen as an attribute of the partner.

Expectations are usually high regarding long-term relationships but can be rather unrealistic, as is the case with Neptune in the seventh, and while a permanent bond may be consciously sought, a partner is frequently chosen who will shortly sabotage this praiseworthy plan. In a surprising number of cases I have come across marriage or marriage-type relationships literally with a foreigner who represents all sorts of romantic and unfamiliar possibilities but never becomes much more than a stranger. In one case a woman married a foreign national she had only known for a few weeks. After living with (and supporting) him for a year or two he vanished, to reappear occasionally over the next twenty years. That she never got round to divorcing him in all this time suggests a certain investment in a formal tie with an unreliable figure, and it is probable that he lived out her fantasies of a footloose existence which did not tally with the values she identified with.

Where the roving Jupiterian quality is experienced as part of oneself, relationships can soon lose their sap. They do not, however, usually leave a lasting bitter taste, for the old expectations soon assert themselves again. Obviously it is possible to find a relationship in which both partners move on together, but this means a felicitous choice of a travelling companion. It involves living a little dangerously, but Jupiter can thrive on danger.

## Jupiter in the Eighth House

The eighth house is a place of death and mysterious transformation, of fusion and fission, sexuality and breakup, of things which are hidden and things that do not entirely belong to us. With Jupiter in this house the path that leads to wider understanding runs through the depths, and that may mean through sexuality and emotional turmoil (George Sand, for example), occult teachings (Elizabethan astrologer John Dee) or the unconscious (Arthur Janov). One woman with this placement had found giving birth a particularly joyful and meaningful experience, and I would not be surprised if it sometimes found expression in murder.

What Freud called the subconscious was a dumping ground for unwanted garbage from consciousness. It was Jung who gave us the concept of the unconscious as a place of astonishing wealth — Pluto to the Romans was also god of wealth — and of meaning and purposefulness. To Freud, who had Saturn and the Moon in the eighth the images produced by the subconscious pointed to the past, to infancy and the primitive in us. To Jung, with Jupiter in this house, the same images conveyed a sense of promise and guidance; he found the light in the darkness and was thereafter the better able to guide others through it. During the period of psychotic experiences on which much of his subsequent work was based the progressed Moon was passing through the eighth and over Jupiter. Interestingly, the breakthrough of the unconscious followed hard on the heels of the breakup of Jung's friendship with Freud, in which he had a considerable emotional investment, so the element of separation that belongs to this house was also part of the picture.

### Jupiter in the Ninth House

Jupiter in this house, of which he is the undisputed natural ruler, produces the constant seeker and explorer who always sees something more beyond what he or she has already discovered. Where the search is defined as a spiritual one, it often leads people through a succession of different traditions, each in turn embraced enthusiastically and later discarded, and when a particular path is chosen and adhered to there is usually a refreshing ability to keep finding new inspiration within it, so that there is still a sense of wonder and of being on a journey.

A church which discourages personal enquiry is not appreciated by those with a ninth house Jupiter.

There are of course sometimes keen travellers with this placement, though surprisingly few of the best known. It also manifests as an unbounded appetite for pursuing and developing theories and philosophies, as for example in the case of Einstein.

## Jupiter in the Tenth House

The midheaven represents that aspect of us which is most in public view, and I have noticed that people often identify with the sign on the MC even if it is untypical of the chart as a whole. It appears in the face of the shopkeeper we see from across the counter and in the face the politician presents to the television cameras, and it tends to be the face that mother encouraged.

When Jupiter comes up in this interface between self and public it comes across as open and good-humoured, and where public prominence is achieved it can certainly aid popularity, often because the particular vision the individual presents to the world captures the public imagination; this in turn fuels confidence, and it is a position which enjoys the limelight. It is not in itself especially ambitious, though where there is ambition Jupiter can of course inflate it enormously. In such cases there are usually challenges from other planets; Saturn for example can goad Jupiter into seeking ever greater glory and self-promotion. I have seen this placement in several charts of stage children, behind whom there are almost invariably high maternal expectations.

Although Jupiter in the midheaven graces the public image it by no means necessarily indicates career success. As usual with Jupiter there can be considerable restlessness, and a feeling of endless possibilities which may never be realized, one thing after another being tried and found wanting, and no profession seeming to offer the scope or freedom required. A role is needed in which the person can use his or her powers of exploration or ability to see the way forward.

## Jupiter in the Eleventh House

The eleventh house reflects our attitudes towards and experience of any group to which we belong, from society at large to the social microcosm of, say, a club, business organization, or even, in the first place, our family.[2] Planets here tend to manifest in the group context and are often experienced via other group members, and also figure in our ideas about how a group should be organized, in other words our political notions.

In the more casual context those with this placement like to spread themselves among different circles and keep as many social options open as possible. They are usually good at facilitating group participation. It is a popular placement on charts of politicians, and inclines towards political theories of a fairly idealistic nature, with an emphasis on freedom. Though there is often considerable political vision and enthusiasm, those with Jupiter in the eleventh make poor party members as strict adherence to a line laid down is not their style; they prefer to make the rules rather than keep them.

Karl Marx, who had Jupiter in the eleventh in Capricorn, had a vision of society perceived essentially in materialistic terms, in which no man was another's economic slave, based on historical necessity and involving a high degree of organization. For W. B. Yeats, with Jupiter in Sagittarius, the vision was anything but material. His pursuit of the ideal spiritual brotherhood led him through a succession of organizations culminating in the secret Society of the Golden Dawn.

## Jupiter in the Twelfth House

The service required by the sixth house is of an immediate and practical nature, coping with the succession of small tasks that enable smooth running of the machinery. Twelfth house service is of a different order, involving complete and utter availability in which there is no room for self-interest. It is the house of sacrifice, and planets here are never fully to hand for conscious personal use but must be offered, whether we like it or not, to something beyond ourselves. It is frequently strongly tenanted in charts of mediums and psychics who, from no personal choice, find themselves surrendering personal control to allow the passage of something else through them. We are channels through which twelfth house influences manifest themselves.

Jupiter is traditionally the natural ruler of the twelfth house, a fact which was brought home to me when I looked at several hundred members of that most Piscean of callings the acting profession and found that a very high proportion had Jupiter in this house, pushing the more flamboyant fifth house position well into second place. Here, then, is the receptive side of Jupiter, giving expression to all our fantasies, carrier of moods and longings and fears which are not the actor's own but belong to everyone. He or she puts us in touch with the mythical realm, with stories and experiences that are universal, and in the process becomes something much larger than everyday life permits.

The gain with a twelfth house Jupiter is perhaps in proportion to our ability to lose ourselves, and this can be experienced in the traditional places of confinement and isolation, so that there are sometimes experiences of unexpected joy and meaning in hospital or prison when all the normal trappings have been stripped away, and particularly when the planet is well aspected there can be a feeling of mysterious protection. There is sometimes a strong psychic attunement and a susceptibility to prophetic dreams.

**Notes**
1. Robert Hand has also expressed this view of the fifth house.
2. Robert Hand, like myself, has noticed that the role one plays in the family of origin is often reflected in the eleventh house; it is after all generally the first group of which we are a member.

DATA
Noel Coward's correct birth time, recorded by his mother in her baby book, is 2.30 a.m., 16 December 1899, Teddington, England, 51N25, 0W20. The relevant page is reproduced in *Noel Coward and his Friends* by Sheridan Morley, published by Weidenfeld and Nicolson, 1979.

All other charts referred to in this section are to be found in Lois Rodden's *American Book of Charts*, ACS, 1980, except for Edna Ballard's, which is in the same author's *Profiles of Women*, AFA, 1979.

# 15.
# Jupiter in Aspect

## Sun/Jupiter Aspects

As our major source of light, the sun is a symbol of consciousness, climbing up out of the darkness and destined finally to sink back into it. We cannot develop our individual potential without developing the characteristics of our Sun sign or venturing into the house where the Sun is placed, and in that process planets aspecting the Sun play an important part. In whatever we hope to achieve we are helped or hindered by them for they are necessary elements in our self-expression and self-fulfilment.

Jupiter blends well with the Sun as they have much in common: they are both masculine and strive forwards towards greater consciousness — there are solar elements in the Zeus myth; both are associated with kingship; and astronomically Jupiter is the only planet which gives off more energy than it receives. The combination of the two is forward-looking and gives a sense of abundance which tends to flow outwards towards others.

The Sun/Jupiter person is endowed with a sense of the future of things, seeing not merely the plain facts (indeed these are sometimes overlooked or undervalued), but where things might lead, and often has a feeling of being guided and a tendency to follow hunches. There is potential in every situation, but no one is better equipped to spot the opportunities for growth and development than the Sun/Jupiter individual, though in the case of the softer angles there is not necessarily the impetus to grasp such opportunities and bring about change. Those with the trine are usually easily contented and have an enviable trust in their own process and often an uncomplicated religious faith. This aspect also has a reputation for sheer good luck, which seems to justify that trust, and although openness, generosity and buoyancy may play a part in this it cannot always be attributed to personal attitudes or effort.

The harder aspects, particularly the square, and also the conjunction, are blessed with a kind of dissatisfaction which can be extremely productive and creative. It is the urge to reach out, explore, enquire, open doors, a desire at all costs not to be confined or limited, and in fact the Sun/Jupiter individual is not easily limited by life because even in the most miserable circumstances he/she does not readily feel trapped. Whether what is sought is a spiritual or intellectual goal and a greater sense of meaning, or freedom and expansion of a worldly kind, gain and achievement tend to be less important than the feeling of expansion itself, the pursuit and the vision that inspires it. In a predominantly earthy chart and particularly when Jupiter is in an earthy sign, practical achievements or accumulation of substance may be the immediate objectives, and Sun/Jupiter can be insatiable in this as in other areas, but it is the freedom and sense of unlimited potential such material resources bring that is ultimately sought. As Jupiter has an affinity with things of the spirit, these individuals are often drawn to matters which elude proof and measurement and are sometimes considered gullible. Their big dreams are often unrealistic, but may still be a source of considerable inspiration and energy.

What has been attained soon loses interest, and so often does the thing which is hard to attain. Prone to enthusiasm, those with the hard aspects easily underestimate the difficulties involved in the tasks they embark on, and if they cannot carry the day by sheer force of positive energy they can soon run out of steam. Much of course depends on the degree of forcefulness and staying power indicated by the chart as a whole. But enthusiasm is infectious, and people with these aspects — particularly the dynamic ones — are good at catching the imagination of others, inspiring them and gaining support. What they have they are eager to share, for their impulse is to be bountiful. The image of the sower, scattering his seeds with apparent carelessness, but in the expectation that they will grow, is an apt one. Views are often eagerly proclaimed and a certain opinionatedness can be manifested. The preference is for doing things openly rather than in secret, though apparent openness may mask doubts. A flare for self-advertisement is not uncommon.

People with the difficult aspects often look a good deal more confident than they really are. Somewhere inside there is a gap between their sense of what they should be and the person they feel they are. Sometimes this is due to parental expectations which do not quite fit. One of the parents, most often the father, represents either strong principles and spiritual values or some sort of dream of greater freedom, and these the child absorbs so that they take shape as a personal task.

The worst manifestation occurs when, completely carried away by some such vision and having whipped up external support, the person identifies with something larger — the company, the state, the cult, the will of God or whatever — and true individuality and any sense of realism are submerged. This is by no means irreconcilable with success, but can lead to all sorts of excesses and total disregard for the feelings of others.

Any problematic Jupiter aspects can be experienced as what Carter refers to as 'religious difficulties', and such is our reluctance to face our own doubts and inconsistencies that we very frequently project one side of any conflict onto an individual or group in the outside world, whose views appear to threaten our beliefs. I fancy that people with these aspects feel drawn towards spiritual paths with which they are somehow out of synch, but as it is such an important issue for them they can hastily or indignantly dismiss such suggestions. Thus they set themselves the challenge of bringing the individual they really are into harmony with their beliefs — or vice versa.

The development of the use of harmonics in astrology promises a fuller understanding of the divergencies in meaning between different angles. David Hamblin, whose work in this area is well-known, offers the following variations on the general theme of Sun/Jupiter contacts:

> If Jupiter is to do with expansion (of course this is only a code-word to cover the variety of meanings of Jupiter), then it seems to me that Sun-Jupiter aspects are essentially to do with *self-*expansion. The examples given below are all of people with *close* aspects, i.e. squares within two degrees, and other aspects correspondingly closer.

> *Sun-Jupiter squares* (i.e. conjunctions in the fourth-harmonic chart) (=striving towards self-expansion):

> David Lloyd George, Harold Macmillan; also Paramhansa Yogananda (mystic), Robert Wadlow (the tallest man who ever lived: see Guinness Book of Records), Henry Deterding (workaholic oil magnate: see Gauquelin *Spheres of Destiny* p. 86) — and myself (DH).

*Sun-Jupiter semi-squares* (i.e. oppositions in fourth-harmonic chart) (= striving towards manifestation of self-expansion):

Che Guevara, Jawaharlal Nehru; also Krishnamurti, Mohammed Ali (Cassius Clay), Katherine Mansfield, Spike Milligan, Lord Byron.

*Sun-Jupiter quintiles* (i.e. conjunctions in fifth-harmonic chart) (= building *structures* of self-expansion):

James Dean, Robert Redford, Glenda Jackson, Albert Finney, Carol Channing, Tim Brooke-Taylor (one of the 'Goodies'); also Anthony Eden, Shelley, Alfred Hitchcock, Howard Hughes, Louis Pasteur, Galileo, Antoine de St-Exupery.

*Sun-Jupiter deciles* (i.e. oppositions in fifth-harmonic chart) (= seeking structures of self-expansion):

Eleanora Duse (see my book *Harmonic Charts*), Greta Garbo, probably Rudolf Nureyev; also Joseph Goebbels, Herbert von Karajan, Jean-Paul Sartre, Alexandre Dumas, Tennyson.

*Sun-Jupiter septiles* (i.e. conjunctions in seventh-harmonic chart) (= inspired by (the idea of) self-expansion):

Friedrich Nietzsche, Jack Kerouac, James Thurber, Fritz Perls, Christmas Humphreys (writer on Buddhism), Dervla Murphy (travel writer); also Joan of Arc, Michelangelo, Sheila Scott (aviator), Tony Hancock, John Addey, Reinhold Ebertin, Grock (clown).

*Sun-Jupiter semi-septiles* (i.e. oppositions in seventh-harmonic chart) (= *seeking* inspiration in self-expansion):

Charles Dickens, J. B. Priestley, John Milton, Emile Durkheim (founder of sociology); also Einstein, Le Corbusier, Oswald Mosley, Chris Sizemore (multiple personality: original of *Three Faces of Eve*).

Sun-Jupiter noviles (i.e. conjunctions in ninth-harmonic chart) (= rejoicing in one's own expansiveness) (for the ninth harmonic it seems better to talk about 'expansiveness' rather than 'expansion', as the ninth harmonic describes a *state of being* rather than a process of becoming):

Rudolf Steiner, C. G. Jung, Annie Besant, Satya Sai Baba (miracle worker), Helen Keller.

*Sun-Jupiter semi-noviles* (i.e. oppositions in ninth-harmonic chart)

(= *seeking* joy in one's own expansiveness):

Paul Cézanne, Rex Harrison, Henry VIII.

Of course the interpretation of these aspects is affected by the sign- and house-positions of Sun and Jupiter and by other planets connected with them.

## Moon/Jupiter Aspects

The Moon is associated with the triple goddess, whose myths predate the myths of solar deities. She is old, she is what has been there from the beginning, mother. She is embodied in the cycles of nature and the mysteriousness of life, pre-rational, pre-conscious, from whom we come and to whom we return. In the experience of the child, father is something that appears on the scene later if at all. Our lives are initially contained by our mother, and without her, or someone to fill her role we cannot survive for long. She is our early environment, and the first and most fundamental things we learn from her, before we have awareness of our separate identity. If she gets it badly wrong, or something happens to her, our future capacity for well-being is damaged.

Our experience of mothering is reflected in the Moon in the chart; a mode of being is described which we fall into very naturally, when we are not struggling, when we respond — as a mother does to a baby — without reflection. Before we have rational thought we have feeling, instincts, and imagination. The Moon represents a more intimate side of us than the Sun, and on her depends much of our ability to feel accepted and happy.

Jupiter easily makes himself at home in this irrational company — he is after all exalted in the Moon's sign. The trines have a basic inner ease and natural flow of the kind almost invariably associated in psychotherapy with good mothering in the early stages. Only those who have experienced willing devotion to their needs are able freely to offer it in their turn, and Moon/Jupiter contacts generally go with a ready concern for the feelings of others and are abundantly expressive of their sympathy.

In the case of the difficult aspects and even the conjunctions the inner ease of the trines is lacking, and there is excitability and a slightly frantic feel at times, which in mothering terms suggests one who was all over the place, unreliable and prone to trying to compensate by being over-indulgent. Those who have these combinations are often very charming, but are somewhat inclined to lay it on too thick, perhaps because the feelings are unreliable and so are sometimes faked. As with so many Jupiter contacts there is a tendency to bite off too much or promise things in the heat of the moment which are wildly unrealistic. The individual feels comfortable being on the move or in a state of excitement and has difficulty settling down to things, and can be prone to the sort of carelessness and untidiness that results from scattered attention.

In a woman's chart Moon/Jupiter can be lushly feminine and often has a disarming spontaneity and exuberance; typical is the woman who is a muse to the men in her life. Screen goddess Marilyn Monroe is a good example; in her case Saturn squares a Moon/Jupiter conjunction in Aquarius, and it would appear that she flaunted her florid femininity (Jupiter is also in sextile to Venus) in part to escape feelings of rejection and inadequacy. The impression she conveyed was one of utter confidence in her womanhood, but behind the scenes she felt unloved and was unable to have the child she longed for. Moon/Jupiter flamboyance can also tip over into hysteria; Jupiter's lack of respect for bounds may blow up feelings out of all proportion.

Men with these contacts tend to be very emotionally susceptible, and the more consciously they have developed themselves into rational beings, the more helpless they are when caught by a transit to such an aspect. Not infrequent is the sensible type who is prone to making a fool of himself over women. His image of the feminine is colourful, inspiring and unbridled, and when he runs into it — as is inevitable — in the outside world it can quite run away with him. At heart, Moon/Jupiter is romantic, and I have noticed that highly emotive music often provides an outlet for those of either sex whose code of conduct allows little scope for emotional expression.

A strong emotional element is also involved where beliefs are concerned, and where there are problems they are likely to be due to a conflict between gut feelings and what one believes or wants to believe, leading to a certain touchiness in this area. Though the two planets are not inimical to each other, they nevertheless represent the opposite poles of spirit and instinct. For women this can be a particularly important struggle, and a possible resolution to the conflict can be glimpsed in the image of the spiritual mother, whose divine wisdom grows lotus-like from the roots of her feminine nature. One woman with a Sun/Moon/Jupiter T-square followed a particular spiritual practice under the guidance of a male teacher and eventually developed and taught her own specifically feminine form of practice. The mother herself often provides a link with spirituality; Monroe was for some time involved with the Christian Science Church (Jupiter in Aquarius!), and in this she was inspired by an aunt, one of a succession of mother-figures in her life.

## Mercury/Jupiter Aspects

The task of the individual with these aspects is that of passing the broad and often exciting view of Jupiter through the narrow funnel of language. By and large those with soft aspects manage this with greater felicity than those with the hard contacts, but this is not always the case, and Mercury's sign is an important consideration.

There is sometimes a remarkable facility for finding just the right words to get across what is perceived with the inner eye, and ability to communicate in symbols, and these combinations can be found in the charts of a number of poets of a more or less visionary type — Rimbaud, whose chart is printed on page 92, is one. Words seem to come to these people with relative ease, and they commonly write fast, in considerable volume and colourfully. More introverted people often prefer writing to talking, but whether in speech or writing Mercury/Jupiter can offer ideas and images which stimulate the minds of others.

The two planets are debilitated in each others' signs, however, and it can be quite difficult to get them to work well together. The tendency to prolixity is often conspicuous and sometimes mocked. At its most vacuous it is an inability to use one word where two or three will do, and to cover up an absence of any real meaning with an abundance of apparent communication, in other words using language as a form of camouflage, a technique practised by certain politicians. Generally though there is a strong and genuine desire to communicate, but so many possibilities are glimpsed that it is difficult to catch them, or the vision defies entrapment in language that conveys all the speaker sees so that alternative ways of viewing the subject come tumbling out one after the other and there is always something more to say, no obvious point at which to stop. People with these combinations tend to use language as a vehicle for exploration, so that they may be hunting down the meaning as they speak, and though they may be eager to get their insights across, the effect is not always one of clarity. Sometimes, too, more is said than discretion would permit. Writing may also be produced with more ease than discrimination. Sir Richard Burton wrote volumes full of fascinating information, but they would have been more readable with pruning; Mercury/Jupiter likes to allow the words to simply flow out, moving between the general and the particular, and usually dislikes editing. As Jupiter has scant respect for details these combinations can be rather careless.

Each time we learn a new language we extend ourselves, discover a new way of looking at the world, so that language itself becomes a form of travel, and those with aspects between Mercury and Jupiter often have a facility for foreign languages.

As in the case of oppositions between Gemini and Sagittarius there may be a discrepancy between reason and faith, and perhaps it is the urgent desire to make these agree that accounts for the predominance of the conjunctions and squares on the charts of philosophers (see page 132). The frustration engendered by Mercury's need to pin Jupiter down arises from a desire to understand things which defy conceptualization. For the person with these contacts such an undertaking is often a compulsion and can be a lifelong concern.

## Venus/Jupiter Aspects

Jupiter's outflowing nature brings to the social realm of Venus a captivating openness and charm. To those with contacts between these two planets the world provides a never-ending supply of fascinating companions, any of whom is likely to spark off new interests and point the way forward to new horizons. They are usually popular because their interest in other people is unfeigned and they are predisposed towards seeing and responding to the positive qualities in those they meet. It can, however, be disconcerting to someone who has just been flattered by this easy and welcoming approach to find that there is nothing exclusive about it, and that the person who appeared so genuinely delighted at the encounter is now chatting up someone across the room with equal enthusiasm.

Jupiter's usual restlessness and aversion to boredom and confinement operates in this as in other contacts, and even the trine is not particularly noted for its stability in relationships. The Venus/Jupiter individual can be faithful in his or her way provided the door is not tightly shut, and is likely to give a jealous partner plenty of cause for anguish. It is not usually a question of flirtatiousness, but rather of a liking for the stimulation of company.

Even when a close relationship has lost its interest, such an individual seldom harbours or attracts serious resentment and usually manages to keep up friendly contact with former partners.

Such pleasing talents can be made to serve useful purposes, and a certain social opportunism and even manipulativeness can sometimes be observed, but there is nothing mean in this combination and it seldom causes real offence.

A spiritual quality is often sought in a relationship, as is the case with Venus/Neptune, but without the latter's longing to become one with or lose oneself in the partner. In the case of the difficult aspects sacred and profane values may clash, and there is often an attraction to friends and partners whose philosophy of life is at odds with one's own, but this is usually experienced as enriching rather than threatening; limiting companionship to the narrow circle of those of like mind runs counter to the nature of Venus/Jupiter. A client who was experiencing a transit to her Venus/Jupiter square met a potential partner who belonged to another faith. Her co-religionists persuaded her to break off the relationship, but she felt quite strongly that such differences ought not to be a barrier.

It is in the Venus/Jupiter contacts that one most commonly finds the proclivity towards the good life and self-indulgence which is sometimes attributed to Jupiter. Possibilities of endless pleasures open up, particularly where there is a strong Venus or Taurus element in the chart, and these are sought and shared freely and with little sense of guilt. While there is often a liking for luxury, cheaper pleasures, as often artistic as sensual, may suffice, and people with Venus/Jupiter aspects usually know well how to enjoy themselves even without a full purse. There is often considerable pride in appearance and a liking for distinctive clothing, and travel is usually a source of delight and an opportunity for meeting new people.

## Mars/Jupiter Aspects

The combination of Mars and Jupiter is something of an unholy alliance. 'All the Planets except Mars are friends to Jupiter,' says William Lilly,[1] and in mythology Zeus is generally disparaging of Ares and his troublesome activities. When the search for spiritual illumination, for universal laws or for a brighter future is backed by a spirit of competition and challenge, the result is a powerful force for good or ill, and one which easily gets out of control.

As the charts of Teresa of Avila (page 87), Martin Luther (page

74) and Billy Graham (page 78) indicate, Mars can bring passion and initiative to further a spiritual cause, and Christianity — to the distress of quietists — has produced many figures whose mission was conceived in militaristic terms. The whole notion of proselytization has a Mars/Jupiter feel to it, and the religious colonization of 'heathen' territory so popular in the nineteenth century is often described in terms of conquest. David Livingstone (page 59), for whom the challenge of travel and conversion went hand in hand, has a quincunx between these planets, an aspect which is more powerful than is often allowed.

There may be many people still who feel that a 'holy war' is a justifiable enterprise, but a conviction of righteousness combined with a heroic spirit can easily become an excuse for horrible excesses and end up as a philosophy of 'might is right'; all the Nazi charts discussed in this book have Mars/Jupiter contacts. The idea of war as a vehicle for spirituality, however, is of great antiquity, and this view is well conveyed in the *Bhagavad Gita*. In this case there is no question of aggression being undertaken in a spirit of zealous self-righteousness, but rather of valour in battle as a metaphor for courage in the face of the inevitable violence and absurdity of human life. Interestingly, Mars and Jupiter are considered 'friends' in Hindu astrology.

Few of us are engaged in anything approaching a religious war, but very strong feelings can be aroused in the Mars/Jupiter individual where any sort of belief or opinion is concerned. Often there is a readiness to project hostility and/or a desire for proselytization onto respresentatives of differing views, and it requires considerable honesty to recognize in this one's own raw assertiveness and need to try out one's power through the medium of one's views. Given this recognition the clash of swords in debate can still be exhilarating, without it these combinations, particularly the inharmonious ones and the conjunction, can be extremely intolerant and generally react strongly to contradiction. John McEnroe, the temperamental tennis star, famous for his clashes with umpires as much as for his play, has the opposition, forming a grand cross with the Sun and Pluto. Mars and Jupiter share a dislike for restraint, and particularly when Mars is otherwise strong personal desires can be pursued with dedication and disregard for others. There is often an attraction towards risk, speculation and adventure, and personal honour is valued highly.

There is considerable energy in these aspects, and they are second to none in promoting a cause although where they are conflicting a lot of energy can be consumed in ill-considered activity and righteous indignation. There is a tendency to go galloping off in all directions, and 'more haste, less speed' is a proverb worth keeping in mind if one falls into this category.

When Mars is harnessed to the spiritual quest and the battle is fought inwardly there is often a willingness to take up arms against the instincts and personal desires. While this can result in an over-harsh attitude to oneself, travelling in the inner as in the outer world has always been attended by dangers and obstacles, and the courage of Mars/Jupiter combinations enables those who have them to keep on where others fall by the wayside.

## Jupiter/Saturn Aspects

Mars is exalted in Capricorn, which implies that his energy can more readily be contained and structured than that of Jupiter, who has no affinity with earth. On the traditional diagram (see page 43), Jupiter is opposed to Saturn, nor is there any love lost between the two figures in myth. Kronos swallows the infant Zeus, tries to nip him in the bud, and Zeus escapes to usurp Kronos' power. Jupiter's careless love of freedom is a threat to the structures Saturn represents, while Saturn's cold formality blocks Jupiter's improvizations.

When the two planets are in harmonious aspect to each other and are in congenial signs, there is generally an ability to move forward steadily and circumspectly, and to follow insights through to fruition without wasted energy, and this is a great help in achieving ambitions. Jupiter loses some of his exuberance but is also less inclined to go to extremes. The conjunction and challenging aspects in the other hand can be distinctly unpleasant when emphasized in the chart, for here the emnity between the two planets is fully experienced.

In Saturn's world there is no room for surprises; everything is as far as possible planned for and proven methods are used. When this caution meets Jupiter's expansiveness and wanderlust there is great discomfort. Sometimes Saturn succeeds in suppressing or externalizing the power of Jupiter and sometimes Saturn's tendency to act as a whetstone to other planets pushes Jupiter to express himself all the more energetically, so that there is a desperate determination to find freedom or faith at any cost. This can bring out Jupiter's worst side.

The first of these possibilities produces the convinced and often proselytizing sceptic, who never loses an opportunity to ridicule any beliefs not based on 'objective facts'. That there are certain beliefs and assumptions lurking behind his fact system which may themselves be questioned is an issue he tries to avoid. Even Karl Marx did not succeed in keeping Jupiter out. He has the sextile, with Jupiter in Saturn's sign, Capricorn, and Saturn struggling to crystallize in the idealistic and irrational quagmire of Pisces (Jupiter's sign). But the system he created can be seen as a substitute religion with its own catechism and, arguably, tremendous faith in the redemptive powers of the proletariat.

On the other hand, the challenge from Saturn can press Jupiter to prove himself, like Thomas thrusting his hand into Christ's side, and trust with these aspects can be both undermined and in compensation very highly valued. There is a longing for God (or Fortune) to show himself and abolish doubts and fears, followed by repeated disappointments. There seems to be a compulsion to seek out such disappointments through some kind of foolish gamble. The fantasy of finding all one's problems solved through some outstanding experience of grace or stroke of luck exerts great power. Or there can be an emotional see-saw; typically, success in coaxing or coercing oneself into a state of unrealistic optimism or elation is followed by an inevitable crash and a period of depression and meaninglessness.

Equally there tends to be a longing for the feeling of plenty a well-aspected Jupiter can provide, and a desire to be generous while in practice having difficulty in giving anything without thought of reward or the fear that what one offers will fall on stony ground. This can sometimes mean giving with one hand and taking back with the other, or offering gifts to which the giver has no proper title, so that the whole operation is tarnished and unrewarding.

The attempt to deny one's fears and doubts inevitably means that other people and outer circumstances take on these qualities, seeming to deny freedom or spiritual values so that there is constant rebellion and discontent. The attempt to find a philosophical or religious framework may also lead to disappointment as there is a struggle to keep the meaning and enthusiasm alive in the system. It is probably only by accepting and coming to terms with one's own fears and doubts that a sense of meaning and purpose can develop, but this is usually the last solution tried.

## Jupiter/Uranus Aspects

Aspects between Jupiter and the slower-moving planets can be within orb for up to a year, and therefore represent something that whole sub-generations have in common, only coming into prominence on the individual chart when inner planets or angles are also involved. These combinations then suggest at the same time a tendency towards beliefs of a certain kind and particular expansive urges common to a large group of people. They are commonly conspicuous in the charts of religious leaders.

Zeus and Ouranos were both gods of the upper realm, of limitless space and dramatic celestial phenomena. Astrologically both planets and the signs of Sagittarius and Aquarius have a strong preference for independence and freedom of movement, and the combination of the two can be extreme in this respect. The challenging aspects in particular are intolerant of ties and have a strong resistance to settling down. As the chapter on travel illustrates, these combinations are commonly found in the charts of compulsive travellers; there is a craving for change, excitement and exploration, particularly of places where few if any have been before. They are prevalent in the charts of astronauts and early aviators — literal sky travellers and at the same time innovators. It is as if the aim is nothing less than escape from the earth and its limitations. Those with the hard aspects for whom travel is not a possibility often tend to jump from job to job or home to home, not necessarily consciously choosing to do so, yet somehow attracted to unstable situations which prevent them from getting too settled. I have several times known people with such aspects strongly placed walk out of a job apparently on the basis of a sudden whim, though presumably the pressure to move had been building up for some time. One man with the opposition on his MC/IC axis had had fifty jobs in less than twenty years.

When Jupiter/Uranus contacts operate in a more introverted mode they tend to produce beliefs and ideas of a highly unconventional and contentious type, either revolutionary or defiantly reactionary. The brilliantly innovative and controversial psychiatrist R. D. Laing has the two planets conjunct on his ascendant, and Heinrich Himmler (see page 116), whose purpose was to actualize a vision of the distant past, had them conjunct the midheaven. Ayatollah Khomeini, leader of the Islamic revolution in Iran which also turned the clock back centuries, was born under the same conjunction as Himmler, and it must surely occupy a prominent position on his chart. Unfortunately the time is unknown.

As can be seen from the last two examples, it is potentially a highly dangerous combination. Uranus's unwillingness to compromise added to Jupiter's propensity for dogmatic proclamations, and given the resistance of both planets to any form of constraint, can lead to extremes of inflation and fanaticism. The realities of human weakness are easily lost from view and there is often a marked unwillingness to examine personal motives, particularly when the chart is dominated by fire and air signs. Whereas Jupiter takes things on faith, Uranus 'knows', sees a whole plan with compelling clarity, and this certainty communicates itself to others, who are either repelled or swept along by it. In the less extreme cases, and particularly when the aspects are harmonious, there is still a great deal of originality and an attraction towards unusual fields of study and unorthodox (or unfashionably orthodox) religious views.

On the collective level Charles Harvey, following Henri Barbault, [2] connects the Jupiter/Uranus cycle with capitalism and the 'free market economy', i.e. the absence of trading restrictions, and also with political extremism and risk-taking.

## Jupiter/Neptune Aspects

As with the Jupiter/Uranus contacts, Jupiter in aspect to Neptune is not particularly at home on the earth, but here the vision is not of freedom and revolution but of a subtle translation into another kind of reality. Instead of challenging the status quo, the preference is to slip quietly into a more dreamlike or magical view of things; the section on vision (pages 83-98) gives a number of examples.

People with these aspects strongly placed are not usually drawn to situations of power and find responsibility particularly irksome; the Peter Pan type who prefers the Never-Never Land of the imagination to the harsh realities of the 'grown-up' world is common. It is a supremely romantic combination and is inclined towards grandiose fantasies which compensate for the banality of everyday existence. When the chart also lacks earth it is particularly easy to drift off into inner space and lose touch with collective external reality, even to split off a part of oneself, Walter Mitty style. There is usually an openness to psychic phenomena, although this may be in terms of interest rather than personal experience.

Although there are often strong mystical-religious inclinations, there can be a tendency to float from one path or teacher to another, for a kind of universality is sought which goes against the disciplines usually imposed by religious organizations. It is not a particularly dogmatic or intolerant combination and has at best a delightfully ecumenical view of things and an ability to relativize different standpoints, whether or not these are specifically religious.

As with other Neptune contacts, those who have aspects between Neptune and Jupiter yearn to be in a place beyond suffering, including euphoric drug-induced states — what was known in the 1960s as 'blissing out', transportation away out of this world. It is the perfect 'signature' for 'Over the Rainbow', and Judy Garland in fact has the sextile, with Jupiter square the Ascendant and Neptune sextile the Sun. Unfortunately Pluto is also involved and tells a very different story; the attempt to maintain a positive state of mind through the use of drugs was also her destruction.

## Jupiter/Pluto Aspects

The god of the heights and the god of the depths have little in common. To Jupiter all is possible, to Pluto everything at some point comes to an end. Individuals with the two in aspect cannot enjoy for long Jupiter's promise without coming to terms with the darkness; where they reach out in hope and anticipation a shadow falls. A woman with the conjunction could only recall childhood experiences of church with a shudder; the walk through the graveyard had made a much deeper impression than the promise of salvation. At bottom there are two ways of coping with this juxtaposition, either to split the two things apart and be forever torn between them, or to attempt some sort of synthesis.

Christianity on the whole has encouraged the split, the pursuit of the bright and heavenly and the flight from the devil. The conjunction in Billy Graham's chart and the frequent recurrence of this polarity (Jupiter/Pluto, Sagittarius/Scorpio) on charts of other passionate religious leaders find expression in a life dedicated to saving people from eternal damnation and from that which threatens to destroy faith. The same split can be experienced in terms that are more philosophical than religious, and in either case there is a risk of paranoia, a sense of threatening persecution from those whose views are perceived as destructive or nihilistic.

Where such a split cannot be maintained, the simple faith that Jupiter loves runs into severe problems, and the experience of the collapse of spiritual values or beliefs in progress results, often quite early in life. Something of this kind befell the explorer Stanley (see page 63) when his early religious upbringing failed to sustain him through the encounter with a brutal world.

One of the results of this kind of experience can be a deeply rooted suspicion of all that Jupiter represents, a tendency to sniff out hypocrisy which can amount to cynicism. Sometimes, however, the abandonment of hope or the proximity of death clears the way for some kind of spiritual renewal, the experience of light in the darkness. The faith that results from this is one that has been forged in the fire and is based on the acceptance of death or impermanence rather than a simple message of hope.

The path to meaning and illumination may involve actively embracing what is dark, hidden or even destructive, and there is often an attraction with these contacts towards magical and occult practices and the powers they can confer. Jim Jones, who had the conjunction, found his own synthesis by creating a cult which involved the literal death of the believers. Religious experiences induced by drugs also seem quite frequent, although drug-taking is not usually spoken of in connection with Pluto. Richard Alpert (Baba Ram Dass) and Timothy Leary, who were largely responsible for the LSD cult of the 1960s, have the conjunction and sextile respectively, and Leary, 'the man who turned on the world', does not even have a very strong Neptune. A clue can be found in the adoption by these acid priests of the Tibetan Book of the Dead as a guidebook: the basis of their revelations was the deliberate obliteration of ego-consciousness, a chemically induced death experience.

Another tendency that seems to be connected with these aspects is what might be called the 'Cassandra syndrome'. I have encountered several people with them who have premonitions or prophetic dreams limited to the theme of forthcoming deaths. Oswald Spengler, the philosopher who predicted the decline of Western civilization, had an exact semi-square.

Perhaps the most constructive solution, though by no means an easy one, is that proposed by C. G. Jung, who had an exact quincunx, and Jupiter in the eighth. For him all optimism about personal or collective progress involved taking account of the shadow, that often threatening counterpole to our conscious aspirations which cannot be redeemed and is another name for the devil.

**Notes**
1.  William Lilly: *Christian Astrology,* Regulus, 1985, p. 65 (orig.
    edn 1659).
2.  See M. Baigent, N. Campion and C. Harvey: *Mundane
    Astrology,* Aquarian Press, 1985, Chapter 6, especially
    p. 186f.

# 16.
# Transits and Progressions

One of the things that stirred my interest in Jupiter was my disappointment over a series of Jupiter transits that brought experiences other than I would have wished myself. My rather naive assumption had been that transits from the Great Benefic must bring joy; instead three transiting conjunctions brought the death of someone close to me, the breakup of a relationship and an illness, all of which were extremely unpleasant at the time.

Jupiter transits are unpredictable; sometimes a thunderbolt strikes, sometimes life takes an unexpected upturn, sometimes very little seems to be happening at all, Whether such a transit is experienced as pleasant depends more on the natal configuration touched than anything else, as transits and progressions are the channels through which the natal chart becomes living experience. Consequently, if a primarily well-aspected planet or angle receives a transiting conjunction from Jupiter, it is highly probable that the experience will be enjoyable, with exciting new prospects opening up in an obvious fashion.

Transiting *trines* from Jupiter are in themselves generally times of ease, though they do not usually coincide with times of significant change. Transiting squares and oppositions from Jupiter are more disruptive. They are usually accompanied by a great deal of agitation and impatience. There is a tendency to get things blown up out of proportion, and often an impulse to kick over the traces or try something new, to take a risk, a feeling of 'the hell with it!'. It is easy to go over the top at such times and do or say things that will subsequently be regretted, and sometimes there are even accidents, especially where Uranus or Mars are involved. Having said that, such shake-ups are often seen as liberating in retrospect, enabling the person to move on as would have been impossible with a more cautious approach. In any case, unless these transits accompany more weighty ones they are not usually of great importance. Occasionally, where the sixth house or Chiron are involved there may be health problems, and swellings, cysts and the like are Jupiterian favourites.

The truly important Jupiter transits are the conjunctions, and it may be useful to consider each one as the beginning of a new twelve-year cycle. The idea of a new beginning or an opportunity for future development is the key, as Jupiter sows rather than harvesting and is orientated towards the future. A Jupiter transit is an opening through which something new can enter so that, for instance, it is common to meet someone who will play a significant role in one's life under a conjunction with Venus. Often there is little more than a glimpse of new possibilities and then, especially when there is no retrogradation and the transit is quickly over, it is easy to miss its significance. Whereas we are usually only too grindingly aware of a Saturn transit, it is enormously helpful to be able to look at what is happening under a Jupiter transit intuitively, symbolically, with an eye to where it might lead; there is always some sort of pointer towards possible future directions. A Jupiter transit to the midheaven, for example, may mean career advancement through a new job, but often it is no more than a new idea for future development in this area. Such a possibility may come to nothing if one is unable or unwilling to develop the idea. There may be an immediate burst of enthusiasm that rapidly wanes.

Jupiter transits can awaken, unblock, release energy. They are often present at the time of a death, one's own or that of someone close. This suggests that death is experienced as a deliverance from bondage or suffering or a going beyond, and when a Jupiter transit accompanies the death of another person, despite the grief there is usually an unlocking of the energy invested in that individual that frees one to move in a new direction. A woman whose father died with Jupiter conjunct her ruling planet (and very little other indication) suddenly found herself able to leave a long-problematic marriage with a man who in fact embodied the negative qualities of her father. She realized that the marriage had in large part been a misguided attempt to win back her father's approval. Now entirely new possibilities were available to her that she had previously been unable to envisage.

Where Jupiter transits coincide with difficult experiences of any kind they can have the effect of jolting a person out of a rut. Sometimes it may be an accident or illness — transits to the ascendant are rather prone to this — but whereas an illness under a Saturn transit usually incorporates a lesson in looking after one's body, under a Jupiter transit it tends to be a disguised opportunity for developing something new. A man who had a minor accident under such a transit found that by being forced to stop working for a while he had the space to think up a new project that led him in an unexpected direction.

Some Jupiter transits are very elusive. It is always a good idea to keep an eye on one's *dreams* at such times, as these may foreshadow things to come, and there can be other experiences of a rather subtle nature. I recall a transit of Jupiter to my Moon in Sagittarius which coincided with a day in which I experienced an extraordinarily liberating state of being, a kind of openness which was new to my adult life. Next day the door had slammed shut again, but it left me with a lasting sense of trust that such a state could be returned to, and clues as to how this might be brought about. On the day of this experience I also had an encounter with a woman who encouraged me to develop my work in a particular, and decidedly lunar, direction.

While on the subject of Jupiter transits to the Moon, I was told recently[1] that transits and progressions involving these two planets had in several cases coincided with conception, and I have since come across other examples. I have not been able to collect further data at this point, but the symbolism is just what one would expect from Zeus's escapades, and it is a new beginning followed by rapid growth in the womb. I have also on several occasions noticed Jupiter transits in the man's chart at such times. An Indian astrology book in my possession[2] recommends that sexual activity aimed at conception should take place when Jupiter aspects the woman's Moon, though it is not entirely clear whether this is to induce conception as such or whether it is to promote a good birth or a healthy or fortunate child.

Jupiter also stirs things up in each successive house as he continues his 11.8 year cycle round the zodiac. Some ideas of the sort of thing to expect are given by Stephen Arroyo in *Relationships and Life Cycles*.[3] I find that people with Jupiter strong in the natal chart are more generally tuned in to his passage through the houses and experience an unfolding or expansion in each area in turn, while for others his transit is felt strongly in some houses and only slightly in others. If progressions and other transits bring into focus a particular area of life and Jupiter enters the corresponding house there can be a great surge of activity. Someone with a fairly long-term progression to Mercury, for example, launched into a flurry of teaching activity when Jupiter passed into the third. As with all transits I find that the time of crossing the cusp into a new house (Placidus) is particularly prone to bring up issues germane to that house, and also the time when it lands on a planet in the house.

The least conspicuous transits through the houses seem to go with a kind of hopefulness or wishfulness regarding the house's affairs, which often leads to nothing tangible — fantasies, say, of making a lot of money when Jupiter is in the second, thoughts of taking up painting when he is in the fifth. At other times a real watershed is indicated, such as moving home with Jupiter on the IC, starting or breaking up a relationship when he enters the seventh or moving into a new circle as he goes into the eleventh.

Transits and progressions *to* Jupiter, which are of course particularly important to those with Jupiter prominent natally, can trip off any of the sorts of experiences of which examples have been given in this book. They may involve travel and the need to explore; religious experiences; visions, dreams and intuitions — Martin Luther King had progressions of both Sun and Moon to Jupiter at the time of his famous 'I have a dream' speech in Washington, and Neptune was also involved; opportunities for material expansion; academic achievements, which of course generally open doors to further studies or career opportunities; the urge to gamble, which may or may not pay off. Very often one's philosophical or religious outlook becomes important at such times, whether because one feels the need to seek out some underlying law, or because one's views are challenged or undergoing change. A whole new vision of the way things are can open up.

The most difficult transits to Jupiter tend to be those from Saturn and Pluto, which are often experienced as depressing or imprisoning. Hopes are dimmed, possibilities close down, beliefs demand examination, or there can be an immense struggle to pin down something one has glimpsed; Einstein was working on some of his most far-reaching theories as Saturn crossed and recrossed his Jupiter. These are times more suitable for reflection than enjoyment. A keen traveller set off on a journey when Saturn conjuncted her Jupiter in the ninth, rather against her better judgement; she had a feeling that she was 'forcing it', that it was somehow the wrong time. Her vehicle broke down five times on the way to the cross-channel ferry as if to underline the point, but she carried on. There was no disaster, but throughout the journey she was depressed so that it felt like a waste of time. It would no doubt have been more fruitful to stay at home and look at the cause of her depression which quite likely had to do with the fading of religious convictions she had fervently held for some years. Others who undertake journeys under Saturn transits leave despite a feeling that things are holding them back, so that the hoped-for sense of freedom and exhilaration is not experienced. Travelling ideally requires an open frame of mind, a certain expectation that something good is going to turn up, and these are usually lacking under Saturn or Pluto transits to Jupiter. They are definitely deflationary.

Perhaps it is wise to bear in mind as transits and progressions to Jupiter approach that when we are *in* our Jupiter we can get swept away by the experience of something bigger, better, more important. It is elating (elate means *carry away* or *lift up*), like a dream of flying, and we don't want to come down. With our eyes gazing into the distance we may be overlooking something near to hand.

## Notes

1. Indirectly by Pat Harris, a Faculty diploma holder and practising astrologer.
2. M. Ramakrishna Bhat: *Fundamentals of Astrology*, Motilal Banarsidass, Delhi, 1967, p. 113.
3. Stephen Arroyo: *Relationships and Life Cycles*, CRCS, 1979, p. 186.

# Index